PATRICIA BERRY

ECHO'S SUBTLE BODY

Contributions to an Archetypal Psychology

Second, revised and expanded edition

SPRING PUBLICATIONS

PUTNAM, CONN.

Published by Spring Publications, Inc.
Putnam, Conn.
www.springpublications.com

Second, revised and expanded edition 2008

Cover design by white.room productions, New York

Printed in Canada

Library of Congress Cataloging-in-Publication Data

Berry, Patricia.
    Echo's subtle body : contributions to an archetypal psychology /
Patricia Berry. – 2nd rev. and expanded ed.
    p. cm.
Includes bibliographical references.
ISBN 978-0-88214-563-1 (pbk. original : alk. paper)
1. Archetype (Psychology) 2. Psychoanalysis. I. Title.
RC506.B43 2008
616.89'17–dc22
                                2008043083

⊗ The paper used in this publication meets the minimum requirements of the
American National Standard for Information Sciences – Permanence of Paper
for Printed Library Materials, ANSI Z39.48–1992

CONTENTS

Prefatory Note   5

Woman

I   What's the Matter with Mother?   9
II   Neurosis and the Rape of Demeter/Persephone   23
III The Dogma of Gender   38

Dream

IV   An Approach to the Dream   55
V   Defense and Telos in Dream   78

Poetics

VI   Virginities of Image   93
VII Echo's Passion   107
VIII Hamlet's Poisoned Ear   119
IX   Stopping: A Mode of Animation   136

Shadow

X   On Reduction   151
XI   The Training of Shadow and the Shadow of Training   171

Rules of Thumb Toward an Archetypal Psychology Practice   181

Prefatory Note

As I look back over the thirty-five year span attested to by these papers, I am struck with how many of the themes that occupied me early on, even at the very beginning of archetypal psychology's first rumblings, continue to vex. The concern and perhaps uneasy relationship with matter continues to fix my attention. The problem with generalities and concepts versus specifics and particulars still concerns me. An effort to formulate how substance, concretism, "reality" work into, alongside of, and within a background of what Henry Corbin called the *Mundus Imaginalis* is for me fundamental. The papers here contained represent my foundation in archetypal psychology. They were the means by which I came to understanding, or more precisely, was able to construct a means by which I could understand what was then a new depth-psychological way of thinking. My hope is that this reprinted edition will continue to serve a useful purpose in the literature of archetypal psychology and aid students in exploring some of its precepts.

P. B.
West Bath, Maine
July 2008

WOMAN

I

What's the Matter with Mother?

If there is any concept that we in psychology have overused, it is that of the Mother. And we have blamed her extensively. At one time or another, in one way or another, we have used her to explain each of our pathological syndromes: our schizophrenia as a double-binding by her; paranoia, an inability to trust because of her (a need to tie our thoughts into rigid systems in compensation for her lack of order); hysteria, a tendency to oversensitize without feeling because of the wandering womb (her womb) in our bodies.

In light of the frequency of these explanations, I began to ask myself – so what's the matter with mother? What's the matter that makes her so useful particularly in psychology's explanations?

In order to explore this question, let us begin by turning it slightly to what mother's matter is – what the content of mother is. And let us focus on the Great Mother of our Western mythological tradition, as described by Hesiod in his *Theogony*. Hesiod honors the Great Mother Gaia, Earth, as the original divinity and progenitor of all the other divinities – all those many forms of our psychic possibilities, forms of psychic awareness. For all these, Gaia lays the original ground.

According to Hesiod, first there was Chaos, a formlessness, a nothingness. Then there was Gaia, Earth: the first form, the first principle, a something, a given.

But inasmuch as Creation takes place continuously – every day our psychic experience is created, our emotions and moods are given form –

rather than tell Hesiod's creation tale in the past tense, we might more accurately tell it in the present: first there is Chaos, and then there is Mother Earth. Within our experiences of chaos, at the same moment there is contained a specific possibility of form. Or each chaos mothers itself into form.

Now this view of chaos is different from our traditional linear notions, in which form is imposed later upon chaos from without or down from above, conquering and replacing the chaos.

To view this tale, however, as I am attempting, would be to see it as an image – more as a picture than as a narrative – so that the facets of the event (the chaos and forms or Earth) are given all at once. Some interesting things turn up in this image picture that don't show up in sequential narrative. For example, this way of looking sees chaos and the forms as co-present: within chaos there are inherent forms. Each moment of chaos has shapes within it, and each form or shape embodies a specific chaos.

Of course, this way of looking at things also has implications therapeutically. For example, here it implies that one must not rid oneself too quickly of chaotic feelings (by abreacting or primal screaming them) because then one would also lose the forms. Better would be to contain, and even to nurture, the chaos so that its shapes may exist as well. (The image further suggests that our forms cannot rid us of chaos, for where the forms are is also where chaos is.)

I can support what I have just said with matter. For mother, this mothering ground of our lives, is connected with the word "matter." Mother and matter (*mater*) are cognates. And matter has been viewed in two ways – almost as though there were basically two sorts, or levels, of matter.

One level is considered as a universal substrate. And as such it exists only in abstraction. In itself, this matter is unknowable, invisible, and incorporeal. Matter in this sense is itself a kind of chaos or, as Augustine describes it, an absence of light, a deprivation of being.[1] So

---

1 Augustine, *Confessions* XII.3.

this view of matter holds it to be nothingness, a negativity, a lacking. Now the second view builds upon this first view.

The second sort of matter is not only the most nothing, but also the most something – the most concrete, tangible, visible, bodily. Augustine calls this matter "the Earth as we know it" and contrasts heaven, which is nearest to God, with this Earth that though most concrete is nevertheless nearest to nothing. [2]

There is within the idea of matter a paradox. Matter (and by extension Mother Earth) is both the most something *and* the most nothing, the most necessary (in order that something can happen) and, at the same time, the most lacking. With this combination of qualities, matter and mother have of course had a rather hard time of it in our Western spiritual tradition. Mother/matter is the ground of existence and yet doesn't count – she is nothing. Archetypally she is our Earth and, at the same time, is always lacking. [3]

When we get close to our "matter," our lower substrates, our roots, our past, the ground from which we came, our lower physical nature, our cruder emotions, it is not surprising that we feel something unsettling, something inferior, chaotic, soiled perhaps. But these feelings are given with the very nature of mother's matter.

Let me tell you of an experience Hesiod had. In the beginning of the *Theogony* Hesiod tells of his conversion to poet, to a man who praised the gods. As he tells it, he was out tending his flocks when suddenly the Muses appeared and berated him for his lowly state. They evoked in him a sense of shame for being only a man of the Earth. Hesiod became then a poet who praised the Muses, but he never gave up being a man of the Earth (a farmer) nor the Earth as his subject. He became instead a more complicated farmer – one who now sang the praises of an Earth that felt to him shameful.

---

2 Ibid., XII.7.

3 It is interesting to note in this regard that Theophrastus describes green, the color of nature, as "composed of both the solid and the void..." Cf. G. M. Stratton, *Theophrastus and the Greek Physiological Psychology Before Aristotle* (Amsterdam: E. J. Bonset, 1964), 135.

Now this would seem peculiar: that a man who was shamed, who was called a fool for being merely of the Earth, would turn now to praise this very Earth for which he felt shame. Or is it that the experience of shame is connected with the experience of Earth, and perhaps shame is a way that may even lead one to the experience of Earth?

Shame is a deep bodily reaction that cannot be controlled (at least very effectively) by the mind. And so shame points to something beyond the will – something of power beyond the human, which we might call the divine. Hesiod was led to experience the Earth as a psychic Earth that though shameful of himself was yet, because of his very shame, more than himself. Within this psychic movement, Earth became a divinity. No longer a mere flat expanse on which to pasture his sheep, as a goddess she became an Earth of many levels upon which his soul (his Muses) pastured as well. For Hesiod she was no longer "nothing-but" a physical ground, a neutral ground without quality; because she was experienced as a divinity, she was experienced psychically so that her matter mattered to and in the psyche.

Had it not been the experience of Earth that the Muses wished to evoke in Hesiod, they might have approached him in another way. They could have brought about his conversion through a visionary experience of great beauty in the distance; they could have asked him in an uplifting moment to lay down his staff and follow them, or whatever. But what was given was the experience of Earth – for Hesiod was to be a poet of the Earth, and from this Earth the entire *Theogony*, in praise of all the gods and goddesses, was to be sung.

Let me read you a Navaho chant that expresses something of the connection between shame and Earth. It goes:

> I am ashamed before earth;
> I am ashamed before heavens;
> I am ashamed before dawn;
> I am ashamed before evening twilight;
> I am ashamed before blue sky;
> I am ashamed before darkness;
> I am ashamed before sun;
> I am ashamed before that standing within me which

speaks with me.
Some of these things are always looking at me.
I am never out of sight.
Therefore I must tell the truth.
I hold my word tight to my breast.[4]

"I am ashamed" – who has not had that feeling when faced with the wonder of Earth? But this sense of shame occurs too when other aspects of "earthy" feeling appear. This happens in analysis when the "chthonic" is constellated: the bug-eyed, toady, twisted, grotesque, slimy, or hulking creatures that bring us startling recognition of ugliness and deformity. Strange that we should feel these creatures as deformed, arising as they do from such natural, earthy levels of the psyche.

We generally try to repress these creatures. If that doesn't work we try second best: to rush them through their transformations as quickly as possible. With a kind of desperation we paint, model, and carry on active imaginations. The principal difficulty is that – in the hurry – we may lose the experience. Because these shameful creatures of the Earth carry the experience of Earth, we lose something of the very Earth we are seeking when we transform them too smoothly. It is a funny psychological fact that being soiled is intimately connected with the experience and benefits of soil.

Fortunately for our mythological tradition, Hesiod's shame connects him to this earthy sustenance and generativist, so that out of her – out of Gaia – proceeds his *Theogony*. Out of her comes the starry sky, the mountains, the depths, the sea.

Strangely enough, all of those so-called masculine regions (starry sky, mountains –Olympus; depths –Hades; sea –Oceanus, Poseidon) have come out of her and are part of her basic matrix. Moreover, she creates her own mate, Uranus. As this Uranus sky is a phallic force proceeding out of Earth, we can see it as Earth's original hermaphroditism. Within the feminine as void, within her as passive, lies a sky-like potentiality. Hence to get in touch with Earth is also to connect with a sky that

---

4 *Navaho Legends*, trans. W. Matthews (Boston and New York: Houghton, Mifflin and Company, 1897), 58.

proceeds from Earth, and the seeds that drop create a kind of original self-fertilization. Not one without problems. But for the moment it is enough to note that sky, mountains, depths, and generations all have their beginnings in primal Earth.

*

In early worship black animals were sacrificed to Gaia Earth.[5] Let us speak for a moment about sacrifice. The very word *sacrifice* means "to make sacred." Thus it is the "black" that is sacred to Gaia and may help keep her sacred. Black: the dark, the depressed, grieving over losses, the inexplicable, the shadowy, the sinful (we might now say).

We now have another hint as to how we may get in touch with Gaia Earth, i.e., through feelings of depression, black moods, losses, and lostness. As shame is a way into the experience of Mother Earth, a related way is the feeling of one's darkest nature and hopelessness – limitations that do not change, complexes that have marked one's personality and will always be as they are, since they are the *ground* of personality, unique and individual. To attempt to lighten these experiences, to get away from these complexes, or to white-wash them with explanations, to rationalize them, would then also be to lose one's possibilities for psychic body, for Earth. These limitations in fact *are* psychic Earth.

Depth psychology serves this ground of the mother in many ways. One is by giving support to the human sense of shame and infirmity, the incomprehensible, the rejected. Psychology not only draws support from the mother's dark depths but, in turn, worships these depths by creating of them a theogony of phenomenological descriptions, systems, and pathological classifications, much as Hesiod created his *Theogony*.

---

5 L. R. Farnell, *The Cults of the Greek States*, 5 vols. (Oxford: At the Clarendon Press, 1907), 3:2. This sacrifice of the black animal (in Gaia's case the ewe) was typical for Hades and other gods in their chthonic, Underworld forms. So we must realize that Earth Gaia is as much at home with the dead and the Underworld as she is with the seemingly more life-sustaining activities of agriculture and vegetation. For her there is no real contradiction between life and death, daily world and Underworld.

And this sense we have of something as pathological cannot be explained away as only due to society, or only because of our parents or the faulty interaction in our families. An idea of pathology, of something amiss, exists in every society. So it would seem to be an archetypal, primary experience. Though of course the designation of *what* is pathological may vary, nevertheless the archetypal fact of it remains constant, through the ages and from culture to culture.

By deepening the experience of pathology, we may deepen our recognition of the mother, the Earth. By this I do not mean experiencing pathology in projection, as something out there. If pathology is archetypal, then by definition we must experience it in ourselves, much as we would any other archetypal quality – *anima, animus,* child... As meanings, they begin in ourselves.

Another of the qualities of mother Gaia is that of immovability. Gaia made things stick. She was the goddess of marriage. [6] One swore oaths by her and they were binding. [7] Mother/matter as the inert becomes now mother as the settler, the stabilizer, the binder.

We still can find this idea of Earth in psychotherapy as that which will settle down a youth who is too highflying, or a woman who doesn't take responsibility for her home, or a man who is too intellectual. What these people need is Earth, we say: the young man we may send off to work on a farm for the summer or urge him to marry; the housewife we may tell to pay more attention to her homelike activities, to put up her own preserves, or work in the garden, or take up knitting; the intellectual we tell to get down to the practical and live life, even at the expense of his "bright ideas" and fantasies.

What we are attempting to cultivate in the psyche of all these people is some ground in which things "matter," happen, become substantial – something into which their life experiences may etch. We are trying to develop the mother within them, their *prima materia,* into a

---

6 Ibid., 15; see also W. W. Fowler, *The Religious Experience of the Roman People* (London: Macmillan and Co., 1911), 121.

7 Farnell, *The Cults* (above, n. 5), 3:2.

supporting matrix, some basic substrate in which psychic movements may take form and gather body.

The curious thing is how literal these therapeutic prescriptions for Earth become. The analysand must actually, literally, do some concrete activity that everybody would agree is "earthy." And yet we all know that when people are even physically involved with the Earth, they haven't necessarily what we mean by psychic Earth. A person can grow his own grains and, at the same time, spin in a mental and emotional space with very little psychic grounding. So it isn't really just physical Earth that connects us to the divinity of Mother Gaia but psychic Earth that has become ensouled with divinity, psychically complicated and, like Hesiod's, touched by the metaphorical muses of soul.

But there is this apparent difficulty in speaking of any kind of Earth, because something about the nature of Earth makes us take it more literally than we take the other elements. If a person lacked air, we would never send him off to learn to fly an airplane.[8] Or if a person's dreams showed that he lacked water, fluidity, we would hardly send him off to learn actually to swim. But when a person is lacking in Earth, we tend to prescribe something rather obviously connected with the Earth, like taking a cottage in the country, making a garden, or chopping firewood ...

Don't get me wrong. I'm not saying that the Muses of metaphor cannot appear in these activities. I'm only saying that they needn't necessarily. The more we insist on enjoining these quite literal earthy activities, the more we may be blocking the appearance of the Muses and a genuine metaphorical Earth arising from within the person, where it makes matter (substance, containment) psychologically.

Depth psychology would seem a discipline in which this reworked and more metaphorical sense of Earth is quite pronounced. It is a field in which we work a good deal for the benefit of, and in keeping with, the metaphorical ladies of soul. And yet even we find ourselves caught in the trap of Earth literalisms. Perhaps it appears in the feeling that our particular orientation is the way – and certainly it begins with our

---

8 See J. Hillman, The Dream and the Underworld (New York: Harper & Row, 1979), 77.

persuasion as to what is most "real." For what's "grounded" and what's "real" tend to be habitually interrelated.

In Jungian psychology, some of us see as most real our personal mother, our childhood, the breasts we actually nursed from as infants. Others of us see what is empirical as most real – those grounds that can be measured and tested. Still others see the social as most real, and so we strive for "genuine" personal interaction and require group therapy, or they may see synchronistic events as most real.

But whatever we take as most real (and partly dependent as Jungians upon whether we inhabit the Earth of London, San Francisco, New York, or Zurich) is what we are using as our mothering ground. And this grounding is extremely important: it is that which gives our thoughts fertility and substance, our therapies, body and results. It is what nourishes our psychological endeavors and makes them matter.

Yet we must not forget the other side of mother's nature (her archetypal being as lack, absence, deprivation). So however hard we work at grounding, each in his own way, we never feel this grounding complete. Always hidden in the very ground we are working is a gnawing sense of lack.

In other words, what we assume as most real, as our mother, is, at the same time, that which gives us a feeling of unsureness. And so we compensate this unsureness with insistence. We insist that one must go back and re-experience childhood, relive the good and bad breast dilemma, for this would give the grounding and the body that is needed. Or we say, if Jungian psychology is not to be lacking, it must be tested and proven to the world. Or, enough of all this flying around in the air talking about synchronicities, we must get down to where people really live with others, in personal emotions and real-life entanglements.

When one orientation fights another, the dispute is fairly serious, for each of us is defending the incompleteness we depend upon as our mother – the ground that has given, and is giving, our activities sustenance. But because we fear her nature as lack, we strive for more support by substantiating her ever more surely. As a solar hero, one fights for the death of the mother's ambiguity by fighting to the death for this increased grounding and substantiation of the mother. Thus identified, one casts aside other, less heroic, modes that would allow the incompleteness of mothering ground to connect with the Muses of metaphor, for whom lacking ground is fertile ground indeed. Metaphor depends upon this sense of lack, this sense of the "is not" with every "is." [9]

We must ask how it is that this literalizing tends to occur with Earth. One explanation lies within the myth. We have mentioned how Gaia created out of herself not only the world but even her own spouse, Uranus. Every night, Uranus, the sky, spread himself down over Gaia in mating. But the children thereby engendered he kept imprisoned in the Earth, which gave Gaia, Earth, great pain, the more so with each additional child, so that by the time the twelfth child arrived (twelve being the completion of a cycle), she plotted an end to this ever-increasing burden. And so she crafted a sickle to castrate Uranus.

This motif of the child trapped in the Earth suggests a way of looking at the problem of literalization. A child, a new possibility, is born, but then this child is trapped in matter. It is imprisoned in the Earth (making this Earth only physical, only literal matter). So the spirit of the new offspring, or the psyche or soul of it, is buried in an Earth that is merely material. Interestingly enough, according to the tale, this materialism gives Mother Gaia herself great pain. She is burdened with each successive offspring buried within her. She is forced to carry what has been projected into her (as literal plans, goals, whatever), thereby losing her more metaphorical possibilities, that part of herself that is insubstantial.

In the myth, the mother eases her burden by turning her destructive potential against this concretism. We might call her in this role the negative mother. She plots castration and devises the means for it. The sickle she invents, however, is fashioned of iron, that metal so important to the building of civilization. So her destructive act is not without benefit and expresses her pain over the way she as Earth is being used.

It could be that when we put too many of our children, our possibilities, into concrete explanations and literal programs, burying their meanings for the soul by living them materially, we are not at all propi-

---

9 As pointed out by R. Romanyshyn in 1977 at the Conference for Archetypal Psychology in Dallas, Tex.

tiating the mother. We are offending her and causing her great pain. We might, therefore, re-examine some of the negative-mother phenomena that appear in dreams and fantasies to see if the negative mother, the castrating mother, isn't attempting (with her belittlement of us, the insecurity and inadequacy she makes us feel) to relieve herself of the concrete demand, the materialistic burden we have placed upon her. What we experience as "castration" of our powers in the world might be that which can move us into a more psychic view of matter. In a curious sense, the effect of the mother's negativity may be to return us to soul. By destroying the superficial surface of that Earth upon which we stand, our literal projections into and upon Earth (achieving more and more – establishing ever more solidly – our materialism), perhaps she is giving opportunity for a deeper ground, a psychic Earth beneath the level of appearance and in touch with the Muses.

★

Now let us look at the children trapped in the Earth in another way. Let us see them as the children "in us" who wish to remain as children buried within the mother, within the concrete. There seem several ways we could do this.

One way would be to identify with the child and then project a goodness, an all-embracing lovingness upon Mother Nature. Then because Mother Nature is all good, I-the-child am also good, innocent, helpless, without Shadow and indeed without much body. I feel no shame – there is no such thing as shame – I am innocent. This state might resemble Hesiod's state before the Muses, and before he was called upon through his experience of awkwardness, separation, and shamefulness to worship the mother. Insofar as a child feels no shame, he is also unable to worship.

Another possibility would be for the child to reinforce his state as child by seeing the mother as all bad. This would be the nihilist perspective and just the converse of seeing the mother as all good. It, too, would deny the mother's possibilities as psychic, complex, worked Earth. This child, scarred by the world's harshness, remains forever the unloved child, but nevertheless still the child.

Another way in which to remain as children buried in the Earth is by dividing experience of the mother into two separate mothers: good mother/bad mother, good breast/bad breast. Although the opposing aspects of the mother are expressed, they have been separated and literalized, seen as nothing-but good here and bad there. And because they are literalized, they tend to be projected into the world as realities out there. This substantiation and projection give them extraordinary power so that I-as-child find myself overwhelmed. Unable to cope in a world so loaded with goods and bads, rights and wrongs, the child languishes ineffectually. Because the world is so important, the child becomes unable; the world's ambiguity becomes the child's ambivalence.

Most often, however, our child abandons his pattern at this point and moves into the neighboring one of hero. Then the darker attributes of the mother appear as the dragon to be heroically slain. Child-turned-hero now girds himself and charges off to do (what turns out to be a rather continuous) battle with the dark mother now become monster.

When heroically opposed, the mother turns monster. The religious sense of her is lost. Her nature as nonbeing, absence, lack is no longer part of her mystery – that which makes her greater than our own narrow senses of life and achievement. Rather, she becomes a contrary force to rule over and conquer. Her Earth becomes replaced by our egocentricity, our illusions of competence, self-sufficiency, ego capability. We deny the Earth's divinity and exchange her ground with its complexities, its twisted chthonic creatures, and shame for our goal-directed, clean, ever self-bettering fantasies of goodness, health, and achievement.

The nature of the hero is to take literally the mother's negativity. Her nature as lack, nonbeing, becomes a real something, an enemy to be fought; her femininity and passivity become a succubus to that heroic life fixed upon progressive achievement. The result is a heroic overachievement and overproduction, which must be countered by equally literal prophecies of doom and destruction. The mother as lack, as negative, returns in prophecies of ultimate, literal catastrophe. Because the Earth is taken so literally, its negative reappears in the forebodings of an equally literal destruction.

The hero's mother complex is characterized by his struggles to be up and out, and above her. And because of his heroic labors to free himself from her, it is he who is most surely bound to her. Better service to the Earth Mother might be to assist her movement down to the deepest regions of her depths. For the mother's depths are the Underworld. Gala's original realm included both the upper realm of growth, nurturance, and life and the Underworld realm of death, limitation, and ending.

We must describe a bit of this Underworld to appreciate how astounding it is that this realm was once part of our mother's Earth.

The Underworld was a pneumatic, airy realm. The beings there, called shades (skiai) or images (eidola) were insubstantial like the wind.[10] It is a realm in which objects cannot be grasped naturally, that is, taken literally, but only felt in their emotional essence. Ulysses, for example, in his visit to the Underworld, yearns for his mother, but when he attempts physically to embrace her finds she is only an immaterial shade. It is a realm of the nonconcrete, the intangible.

And yet an essence of personality is preserved. Cerberus is said to strip away the flesh of persons who enter, leaving only their skeletal structures, those essential forms on which the flesh of each life has been modeled. This sense of essence is also shown by the repetitions that some shades enact (Ixion on his wheel, Sisyphus and his stone, Tantalus and his everlasting hunger and thirst). These repetitions may be viewed symbolically as the characteristic pattern of each individual personality.

The Underworld is colorless.[11] Even the shade of black does not appear except in the Upperworld that sacrifices to it,[12] hence we emphasize the experience of blackness in connection with Gaia, for black is our Upperworld experience of the Underworld, our way into it. But once there, one is, so to speak, deeper than one's emotion. One is beneath

---

10 F. Cumont, *After Life in Roman Paganism* (New Haven: Yale Univ. Press, 1922), 166.

11 K. Kerényi, *The Gods of the Greeks* (London: Thames & Hudson, 1961), 247.

12 Cumont, *Roman Paganism* (above, n. 10), 166.

the depression, the black mood, by having gone down through it to the point where it no longer is. When we no longer cling to the light, blackness loses its darkness.

In the Underworld one is among the essences, the invisible aspects of the Upperworld. The word "Hades" means the invisible or the "invisibility-giving."[13] It is that realm deep beneath the concrete world and yet somehow within it, in the same way that the seed is within the fullgrown plant, and yet is its inherent limitation, its structure, its *telos*.

But there came to be a split between the Upperworld aspect of Gaia's Earth and its Underworld aspect. Her upper realm became Ge-Demeter while the under realm became Ge-chthonia and relegated to Persephone.[14] The Upperworld became a Demeter realm of concrete, daily life, devoid of the spiritual values, the sense of essence and the dark (and beneath the dark) carried by her Underworld daughter, Persephone. For reunion with this Underworld daughter, Demeter suffers inconsolably. And we, without a religious sense that includes and connects us with the Earth's depths and essential insubstantiality, suffer as well.

In our efforts to establish a solid "real" world and make the mother carry our concreteness, we have lost an aspect of her grounding – a grounding that has not so much to do with growth in any of the more concrete senses of Upperworld development. More psychologically futile is our invisible mother in the Underworld: the Persephone who rules over the soul in its essential, limiting, and immaterial patterns; and that original mother of all – Gaia – she who is Earth, and yet without contradiction, that deeper ground of support beneath the Earth's physical appearance, the nonbeing beneath and within being. Our fruitfulness – our fecundity, our sense of what "matters" – has its roots in our very unsureness, in our sense of lack.

---

13 Kerényi, *The Gods* (above, n. 11), 230. H. J. Rose suggests that the name Hades may also be derived phonetically from "the Unseen." (*A Handbook of Greek Mythology* [London: Methuen, 1965], 78.)

14 Whereas Demeter, like Gaia, appeared imagistically as the ripened or ripening corn, she never appeared in connection with the seed in the ground or with Underworld figures as did Gaia; see Fowler, *The Religious Experience* (above, n. 6), 121. This absence of Demeter's Underworld aspect makes an Underworld Persephone "necessary."

II

Neurosis and the Rape of Demeter/Persephone

My particular interest in myth is to understand its workings in people's lives, in psychological practice, and in psychopathology. C.G. Jung laid the groundwork for all this with his original understanding of myth as the content of the psychoses. Then in *Symbols of Transformation* he went on to draw parallels between processes in mythology and in schizophrenia. I am interested in making the same sort of parallels between mythology and the more humdrum processes in neuroses – particularly defenses and resistances. This seems to me useful since we deal with such neurotic processes primarily in terms of Freudian "defense mechanisms" on the one hand and personalistic process interpretation (transference reactions) on the other. To view these defenses archetypally gives added ground and dimension and helps to extend Jung's insight with the psychoses, and indeed all psychic phenomena, to the more specific workings of neurotic patterns. But first the job is to locate more precisely where certain patterns belong archetypally and may even be necessitated by a myth.

Demeter is an example of a mythic figure evidencing neurotic behavior. In approaching this figure and this myth, however, I shall not be doing an "interpretation"; I shall not be dealing with the events in the story step by step, making them coherent and "fitting" as a narrative or case history. Rather, I shall read the story as a mythical image,[15] as

---

15 See below, "An Approach to the Dream" (esp. on Simultaneity), where I attempt to lay the groundwork for this approach to products of the imagination.

though there were no beginning, no end – as though it all went on at once, and forever.

Demeter consciousness has to do with "life," the life of the seasons, the growth of the grain, agricultural vegetation. She is an Earth Mother, [16] but in one important sense a limited one: she suffers an extreme loss within her very motherhood, the rape and abduction of her daughter Persephone. Moreover, this loss is aided by the greater, older Earth Mother Gaia (who grows the seductive flower for Hades) – as though nature at the Gaia level understands the rape as necessary. [17]

Now in order to know what this attitude of Gaia implies, we have to get some idea as to what a rape into the Underworld is all about. But I don't want to go into mythological amplifications concerning the

---

16 According to Kerényi, The Gods (above, n. 11), Da was an ancient name for Ga or Gaia, so that Da-mater (later becoming Demeter) had to do with the quality of Earth Mother. On the other hand, M. P. Nilsson, in Greek Popular Religion (New York: Columbia Univ. Press, 1940), quoted by Guthrie below, maintains that Demeter is the goddess of corn rather than of Earth or vegetation in a more general sense. In The Greeks and their Gods (Boston: Beacon Press, 1951), W. C. K. Guthrie refutes Nilsson by asserting that "such evidence as we have concerning the religion of the pre-Greek peoples of the Ægean basin suggests the widespread worship of a goddess who was regarded as the mother of all life, vegetable and animal" (283 n). M. Grant, in his Myths of the Greeks and Romans (London: Weidenfeld and Nicolson, 1962), also supports a more general view of Demeter as Earth (128). For the purposes of this paper, and in keeping with Kerényi, Guthrie, and Grant, we shall regard Demeter as a goddess of vegetation (corn as pars pro toto for agricultural vegetation).

17 K. Kerényi, "Kore," in Essays on a Science of Mythology: The Myth of the Divine Child and the Mysteries of Eleusis, with C. G. Jung (Princeton Univ. Press, 1969), says: "the patient earthly endurance of the absolute mother is wholly lacking to her [the maiden]. It is not without reason that Gaia aids and abets the seducer in the Homeric hymn. From the Earth Mother's point of view, neither seduction nor death is the least bit tragic or even dramatic" (136). In the "Hymn to Demeter" (The Homeric Hymns, trans. C. Boer [Putnam, Conn.: Spring Publications, 2003]), the text reads: "... narcissus even/which Earth,/as a trick,/grew/for this girl,/as a favor for/Him Who Receives So Many,/and with Zeus/allowing it/(its brightness/was wonderful!)/.../she stretched out/both her hands/to pick/this delightful thing./But the earth,/wide with roads,/opened up!/... and out came/He Who Receives So Many" (89–90).

Underworld – it's been done elsewhere. [18] Let me just say I understand the Underworld as the realm of souls. As a matter of fact, for the Homeric Greeks the psyche was found only in Hades. The Underworld – not life – was the place of psyche. We could easily get into a dualism about this and see the Underworld as soul and the surface world as physical or mundane life. So it is important we remember that the Earth Mother Gaia, who supports all physical life, was at the same time an accomplice to Hades. For her the Underworld is also part of nature. From this Gaia perspective, we can then see Demeter and Persephone as a pair, that is, as aspects of each other – so that when one of them does something, the other also shares in the activity. [19]

In order to care for psychic growth and vegetation, Demeter/Persephone must discriminate among it. Or perhaps Demeter's caring is a natural discrimination, though most probably not along the lines of Linnaeus (genus, species, and gender), but more in terms of place

18 See J. Hillman, *The Dream and the Underworld* (above, n. 8), for a more complete description of the psychic attributes of the Underworld. Cf. also Rose, *Greek Mythology* (above, n. 13): "All that is left [in the Underworld] is the psyche or breath-soul ..." (79).

19 This near-identity between Demeter and Persephone has been shown in many other ways as well. In "The Psychological Aspects of the Kore" (*Science of Mythology*, above, n. 17, 162), Jung arrives at a general statement of mother-daughter unity: "We could therefore say that every mother contains her daughter in herself and every daughter her mother, and that every woman extends backwards into her mother, and forwards into her daughter." Kerényi ("Kore," ibid., 137) assumes the Demeter-Persephone unity because "the fluidity peculiar to the original mythological state presupposes a oneness with the world, a perfect acceptance of all its aspects ... by entering into the figure of Demeter we realize the universal principle of life, which is to be pursued, robbed, raped, to fail to understand, to rage and grieve, but then to get everything back and be born again." Then later, in the "Epilegomena" (ibid., 178–79), Kerényi states: " ... our insight into the fundamental identity of Demeter and Persephone ... is based on psychic reality and on the tradition that testifies to the existence of this psychic reality in antiquity." He then quotes W. F. Otto as saying, "Demeter, mourning for her daughter, is mourning some nature that is essentially akin to her, that makes the impression of a younger double." The entire position of their unity is worked out at length in Kerényi's major study on the subject, *Eleusis: Archetypal Image of Mother and Daughter*, trans. Ralph Manheim (London: Routledge & Kegan Paul, 1967).

and season, what grows where and when. Natural objects are particulars, which require particular soil, climatic conditions, and care.
With this sort of discrimination natural products are perceptively separate from each other, even while they may grow alongside each other.
As Persephone is at home with Underworld essences, she perceives
surface-world differences. [20] By this I mean that the appreciation of differences in Demeter's realm of nature is also a perception of essence in
Persephone's realm – where essence is the "unseen," the hidden seed of
the pomegranate, or the "invisible." [21] In this way, to notice Upperworld
differences is at the same time to perceive by means of an Underworld
consciousness of invisibles. Thus what we have called perception is not so
in the ordinary sense of the word, but a deepening of concrete objects by
perceiving them as germinations of the realm of Hades. From this perspective, the concrete natural world, unlike the mystical denial of it, is
the very way and expression of soul. Demeter/Persephone sees so deeply
into objects that she sees through them. [22] And when one sees so deeply
into nature, the life of the sprout above the ground takes on a depth significance beneath the ground. The sprout and its fruits are significant
and what one does with them is significant.

Let us try to get a bit closer to this sense of significance. It is first of all
deeper than, more perceptive than, an "enthusiasm" for nature – a hefty
denim girl ecstatic over her wheat germ. I question if this wow!-and-

---

20 Though their reasons vary, classicists tend to agree that Persephone
plays an essential role in the actual life of the crops. Most of them explain this
naturalistically, as though Persephone were herself a plant and must therefore
spend a third of the year, the time when the fields are empty and barren, beneath the Earth (cf., for instance, Guthrie [above, n. 16], 284). To give a more
psychological explanation of Persephone as plant life would seem to require
a metaphorical observation of the plant itself, to ascertain those Underworld
qualities inherent in it throughout its stages of development. Mere organic
death at the end is too literalistic a reduction of Underworld qualities, which
can be said to be present within all life, not just in its running down.

21 See above, n.13.

22 Hekate, the third female component within the tale, is called *phosphoros*,
the light-bringer (Kerényi, *Science of Mythology* [above, n. 17], 110). Hekate thus
suggests the *lumen naturae*, the light of nature.

wonder approach to nature is really it. Demeter is, after all, primarily a depressive goddess. At one point, it is true, she leaps in Maenadic delight at the return of her daughter,[23] but that's short-lived. Her basic, underlying mood is heavily earthy and under-earthy. Not for long is she an enthusiast, nor I believe is she one who searches for "meaning" and "truth." She searches merely for her daughter – that Underworld component that belongs by birth to her. And with this kinship tie comes her significance and the significance of everything she does. Whether she cooks with this kind of ingredient or another makes a difference – not because one is designed to dispel the "unnatural" effects of civilization – but because the taste is different – and that *does* make a difference. But again significance does not have to do with meaning. It is not because some lore is attached to thyme and another to rosemary, but because to Demeter's taste they are *sensually* different. The sensual, daily moments of life when viewed in terms of underlife (death) become discrete and separate, and each moment of sensation becomes significant. There is no way that life may be experienced as "just life," just getting on, making do. Life takes on a significance of the senses. The senses become so wholly life-giving because sensation reaches to and incorporates the Underworld.

But we must return now to our main line of discussion – neurosis. For it is one of those curiosities about archetypes that they appear just as easily pathologically (abnormally) as they do normally. This normality/abnormality of the archetype is useful for neuroses and their therapy. For the idea implies that in one and the same archetypal pattern lie both the pathology and its therapy. If we take seriously the traditional maxim of "like cures like," then once we recognize an archetypal pattern, we know a great deal about curing it. That is, we treat it with itself – by deepening it, expanding it (so that it is no longer so narrowly fixated), and by giving it substance, body (so that it can now begin to carry what it is trying to express). But the difficulty with any neurotic symptom is that not only does it express something (its *telos*, intentional purpose, or finality, as Jung would call it), it also tries to make certain that that goal is never reached (as Adler might have said).

---

23 "Hymn to Demeter" (above, n. 17), 125.

For an explanation of this "self-defeating" situation we might remember Freud's description of the symptom as a compromise solution.
The symptom actually expresses the repressed content. But this expression is partial, a kind of token to unconscious forces, which makes
possible their containment, by or in the symptom. Total repression
would risk total collapse, but this partial repression allows the safety
of a compromise, neurotic containment. Thus the symptom acts as a
safety valve, allowing the continued existence of the repressed. So the
real stigma of a neurosis is that it uses itself to defend against itself,
superficially using its own contents to defend against any deeper entry
into those contents. We might invert the maxim of "like cures like" to
read also "like *defends* against like."

How might such defenses appear in the Demeter style of the psyche?
To begin with, her very suffering may manifest neurotically. It may take
on that "suffering for the sake of suffering" quality or that misery to
avoid deeper pain.

But we must be careful because this need to suffer is also quite genuine. There is a ideological reason for it. Demeter *needs* her Underworld
daughter, and it is through the suffering of the mother that this need is
symptomatically expressed. Her suffering is her compromise with the
rape: her manner of experiencing and refusing it. To put it another way,
Persephone's rape is experienced as Demeter's neurosis. And this neurosis is continually present within the archetype. Since myths are eternal and never fully resolved in life, we may expect certain parts of our
personalities to be in perpetual enactment of some rather disagreeable
mythic kinks. When in tune with Demeter and receiving her gifts, I must
also expect some of the accompanying difficulties and unconscious tendencies of that archetype. Then, too, my need will be always to deepen
teleologically in the direction of Hades, my daughter's realm. Thus I suffer, and yet thus I also resist – for that, too, is part of my mythic pattern.
There is no way *out* of a myth – only a way more deeply into it.

We have mentioned suffering as itself a defensive measure. We might
enlarge that to include the phenomenon Freud describes as mourning.
Freud sees mourning as aggression against the lost object, now turned
inward. Thus I punish myself, and I would add, others, by means of dis-

placement (the mourner or depressive who punishes others, or poisons the atmosphere with his mood).

When we view Freud's mechanism of internalized aggression in a more Jungian way, we immediately see that the introverted aggression accomplishes quite the same thing as would Freud's extraverted idea of aggression. For what is punished is the archetypal component, the daughter Persephone, wherever that happens to appear, externally or internally. A mourning Demeter who has lost the daughter, therefore, hates the daughter and all that Underworld business the daughter now represents. Neurotically, Demeter's consciousness clings all the more fervently (and destructively) to the Upperworld, adamantly denying Underworld attributes such as precision (the house becomes a mess), discrimination (one thing is as good as another – all feelings and all sensations of equal value and thus of no value), sense of essence (things become of value for their superficial, rather than underworldly, attributes), and sense of significance (the ordinary loses its link with the gods, the archetypal, and is therefore "nothing but").

Demeter consciousness becomes depressed, and within this depression we can see many classically psychiatric attributes: she ceases to bathe,[24] ceases to eat,[25] disguises her beauty,[26] denies the future (her

---

24 Ibid., 93: "Nor did she once / plunge her body / in bath."

25 Ibid.: "... and not once did she taste / ambrosia, / or that sweet brew, / nectar, / for she was grieving." H. J. Rose mentions (referred to by Guthrie [above, n. 16], 220) that taboos on food and wine were characteristic of chthonic rites. We might look at the difficulties of food intake, both anorexia and compulsive eating, against the background of these rites. We know also that the pig is Demeter's sacrificial animal. Kerényi (Science of Mythology [above, n. 17], 118) tells an Orphic variation of the rape tale in which a swineherd, Eubuleus (a name also of Hades), is witness to the rape, and his pigs are swallowed up by the Earth along with Persephone. There is also the tale of Demeter who, distraught with grief for her daughter, gets carried away and unwittingly eats Pelops's shoulder (Rose, Greek Mythology [above, n. 13], 81). Here Demeter eats with such abandon that she has no awareness of what she is eating. And when Demeter thinks of immortality it is by means of cooking – the roasting of Demophoon.

26 "Hymn to Demeter" (above, n. 17), 97–98: "she went to / the cities of men / and their grasslands, / disguising her beauty / for a long time / ... /

possibilities of rejuvenation and productivity), regresses to menial tasks beneath her ability[27] (or sees her tasks as menial), becomes narcissistic[28] and self-concerned, sees (and actually engenders) worldwide catastrophe, and incessantly weeps. The depression of Demeter consciousness manifests itself with a certain dry asceticism (no bathing, no eating, no sensuality) and self-denial. But alongside this dryness she weeps with "vain and insatiate anger."[29] So her wetness is in effect dry,[30] an excess of tears that neither moistens nor makes for flow or connection. There is no *anima* in this wetness. It is a kind of continuous downpour that erodes rather than replenishes the soil, making it ever more dry and less fertile.

Another peculiarity of Demeter depression is her tendency to seek refuge among man, the social world, the city.[31] She doesn't go off alone into the woods as might Artemis, or try to prove her self-sufficiency as might Hera, or rush into a love affair as might Aphrodite. Rather, she breaks her connection with the gods and seeks refuge in the *polis*, the world of everyday events: "reality." Thus she may defend herself from the needs of her own deepening with "reality excuses." It becomes "impractical" to tend to her soul. She has no time. It is not her business. She must take care of the children and the household (which chances are she is doing inadequately, with only the surface of herself, anyway). Indeed then, the needs of Demeter's soul begin to cast themselves in ways that actually *are* impractical[32] and antisocial. She perhaps expresses these

looking like / an old woman / who was beyond / child-bearing, / beyond the gifts / of Aphrodite…"

27 Ibid., 101.

28 Ibid., 96: "But goddess, / stop / your own great weeping. / It does not fit you, / this anger that's / so vain / and insatiate."

29 Ibid.

30 That water can dry we find expressed in another story: Proserpina (Persephone) throws water into the face of Ascalaphus, turning him into a bird, an air creature (Ovid, *Metamorphoses* 5.543).

31 "Hymn to Demeter" (above, n. 17), 97: "She withdrew / from the company of gods / and from great Olympos, / she went to / the cities of men / and their grasslands."

32 Demeter consciousness tends to live life in a natural, clockwise direction;

needs in suicide attempts (literalizing death as Hades), in religious conversion (portraying her need for spirit), or by leaving her family, breaking her marriage, and living out in desperation some fling or affair (in a
displaced enactment of her daughter Persephone).

As it is Persephone's narcissism (the flower Narcissus), in the Homeric
tale, which brings Hades rushing up upon her, so Demeter's narcissism
helps connect, and yet depotentiate, Underworld forces. One way we
see this is in the ceaseless self-indulgence of much of her suffering.
Her dry tears erode the soil; her suffering engenders suffering for all
the world; her mourning, mourning. On and on, as though her suffering fed upon itself – and yet where is the sustenance for such feeding,
since everyday life gets worse and worse? It is as though this repetition
were mimetic of another Underworld characteristic – the endless cycle
by which essence is expressed (Ixion on the wheel, Sisyphus and his
stone). [33] In the Upperworld, this endless, cyclical essence is expressed
as repetition. [34] Apparently meaningless emotions are compelled to repeat again and again fruitlessly as though to connect to the essence
beneath themselves – the Hades realm.

Since Demeter's depression takes her toward the realm of man,
rather than away from it, her kind of regression takes her into nearness, neglecting her connections with the divine. By losing connection
with what she is, a goddess, she inflates the personal, so that life's little
messes become of great value. The significance in the small becomes
the small inflated with significance. Demeter's closeness has become
actually a defense against the divine depths and results in a proxim-
ity that is petty, mean, and overly personal. A witchlike character

---

whereas to connect to her daughter she must begin to live in a *contra-naturam*,
counterclockwise manner as well. Kerényi (*Science of Mythology* [above, n. 17],
134) remarks how the rituals "if danced in honor of Persephone, would have to
go as it were in the wrong direction, that is, to the left, the direction of death."

33 For a further list of Underworld repetitions, see Rose, *Greek Mythology*
[above, n. 13], 81.

34 One aspect of neurotic repetition is its partial nature. The act must occur
repeatedly as though to make itself complete. Repetition is a good example of
the symptom as a compromise solution, at once expressing and defending.

appears, [35] and the personal becomes self-important as Demeter sits in her "sumptuous" temple, [36] smothering in mundane events, cut off from Olympus.

Since she is dissociated from both Olympus and Hades, this neurotic pattern may become very destructive indeed. Demeter's earthiness now becomes the weight that smothers every living potential. She conceals the seeds in the ground. [37] Not only does she sever herself from Olympus, but now all connection between man and the gods is threatened. Consciousness is leveled to the grassland, the horizontal, and spirit lies fallow, beneath the Earth. Existence grows barren and fruitless. As Demeter is split from Hades, she now enacts his deathliness – but in her own way, for it is Earth she kills with. To find and reunite with her spirited daughter becomes a matter of psychic survival.

But what brings this reunion about? Or, therapeutically speaking, what are its necessary preconditions? That Demeter suffers deeply and causes suffering for others does not guarantee change for the future. Excluding grace, or spontaneous remission, she could go on like that in her neurosis forever. Of course another archetype might constellate,

---

35 This witchlike character that sometimes manifests itself in the neurotic Demeter condition suggests her tie with Hekate (see above, n. 22). Even the names are connected: Perse, Perseis, Perses, Perseus, and Persaius are also names once used for Hekate and her associates (Kerényi, The Gods [above, n. 11], 113). Furthermore, Hekate had qualities of fertility (Rose, Greek Mythology [above, n. 13], 121), nursing, and nourishing (Kerényi, The Gods [above, n. 11], 113). Also proper to Hekate were the dog, the bitch, the obscene (cf. Baubo, in ibid., 244); she was also the goddess to whom garbage was ceremoniously offered (W. H. Roscher, Ausführliches Lexikon der griechischen und römischen Mythologie [Leipzig: Teubner, 1884–86], s.v.). Since Demeter rejects the Underworld, and Hekate, too, has her Underworld side, some of Demeter's Shadow qualities might be expected to appear in the form of Hekate, "the sisterless." When Demeter regresses into closeness, she may be at the same moment sisterless – both near and yet witchlike, unrelated.

36 "Hymn to Demeter" (above, n. 17), 116.

37 Ibid., 121–22: "For she's thinking about / the enormous act / of wiping out / that weak race / of men / who are born on the earth, / concealing / their seeds / in the ground / and thus annihilating / the honors / of the gods / ... / but she sits, / far away from them / inside a fragrant temple, / and she never leaves / the rocky city / of Eleusis."

giving her relief in that way. But this kind of relief would be more the sort deriving from a "rest cure" or a "change-of-scene" and would avoid delving into the depths of her own particular archetype. The kind of movement we are really interested in would be one from within her own archetype, within her own substance. For this, it would seem first necessary that her compromise container fail. The suffering of Demeter consciousness must become unbearable to that which carries it – her neurosis. The Underworld intentionality of her symptoms must become too much for its surface containment.

Now what would such a failure feel like to Demeter consciousness? It might very well feel like rape. It might very well feel like something happening to her – since it is the last thing she feels she wants and precisely what she is defending herself against. So the phallic force bursts up from beneath, through the ground of her awareness, her Earth defenses, and takes the maiden cherished within motherly folds, life's innocence.

Indeed Demeter consciousness tends to draw rape and violence upon itself. We know of two stories in which Demeter herself is raped. In one, fleeing the advances of Poseidon,[38] she turns herself into a mare – a peculiar transformative choice in that now the rape can be consummated quite naturally: Poseidon in his horse form, and she obligingly a mare. The second tale is one that Demeter fabricates to explain her unfortunate circumstances to the daughters of Celeus.[39] And like all lies, this one contains some psychological truth. In it, she spins an elaborate fantasy of how she has been raped by pirates and carried far away from her homeland. We might certainly say that by way of the rape of her daughter, Demeter was raped from her natural grounding; but it is

---

38 According to Kerényi (The Gods [above, n. 11], 181), the name Poseidon may even mean "husband of the goddess Da" (see above, n. 16, for the connection between Da and Demeter). Furthermore, Poseidon's surname of Gaiaochos means "husband of Earth." Poseidon also carries qualities of Hades and the Underworld: he and Earth are sometimes enemies (he fights her sons, the Giants) – and yet, like Hades, he is also somehow a nurturer. One of his cult titles is Phytalmius, nurturer of plants (Rose, Greek Mythology [above, n. 13], 66–67). Thus Demeter's rape by Poseidon has curious symbolic parallels with Persephone's rape by Hades.

39 "Hymn to Demeter" (above, n. 17), 100–101.

interesting that *she* construes this as horizontal movement (from Crete to Thorikos) instead of the vertical movement that more accurately describes her daughter's rape.

Again Demeter consciousness views events as above and across the Earth's surface, in lieu of the radical, the fearful, shift of perspective that would view these same events as beneath, in depth.

And yet to accept our own rape, downward into the Underworld, is no easy matter, since by definition it must happen *to* us and to that part of us most inviolate – the virgin. Let me qualify this: it is not just any virgin who constellates or necessitates rape, but primarily Persephone, whose devastating innocence and half-conscious teasing lead anyway into Underworld realms, whatever they may be. For other virginal figures, like the goddesses Artemis and Athene, rape would be an archetypal monstrosity, an actual destruction of the archetype instead of a deepening through it. Practically, we might put it this way: rape is a horror, but when and however it is constellated, if it connects to the Demeter/Persephone archetype, then the violation is not only possible, but essential.

We mentioned how for Demeter consciousness the rape must be unbearable. We might add now a second condition: that it be incomprehensible.[40] When the rape happens to her daughter, Demeter can have no footing beneath it. She cannot under-stand (stand beneath). As "Demeter Green Verdure" she deals with the vegetation of the horizontal world. With the rape, her perspective shifts toward the vertical as well – now taking on the depths and heights and the route of spirit. Without the vertical sense, Demeter cannot "stand beneath." She cannot move in terms of depths or levels. Not only depth as "the unconscious," but depth potential as a seed in each moment of life, its metaphorical implications below its apparent sense. But this limitation is a natural and necessary one. Any sort of pseudo-understanding, helping to explain away her state, or rationalizing it into containment, giving her a too easy verticality, would block her participation in the archetype and its profound possibilities.

40 See above, n. 19, where Kerényi stresses Demeter's failure to understand.

This has bearing on our treatment of Underworld anxieties and dream motifs. When such threats are constellated, the worst possible interpretation, in light of the Demeter/Persephone myth, would be to make the value judgment of "destructive *animus*" or "negative Shadow" concerning these figures. In fact, this attitude would lock the dreamer within her virginal state and further her confinement within a superficial, Upperworld rationale. When we make these interpretations, it is because we assume the dark pursuer is out to destroy the dreamer's femininity. Our intentions are really humanitarian and, we think, all in favor of the feminine. But we overlook the deeper layers of the myth which would support the threats as precisely the mode of initiation. The "rapist" may be constellated in response to the dreamer's too-narrow virginity, and his purpose may be to escort her physically into that deeper body which lies beneath all surfaces, the psychic realm.

We have been speaking of "rape" in the broadest possible sense, but now, by way of example, we might look at some dreams in which the threat of rape is cast in the image of a physical threat:

(1) *The dreamer, having done her grocery shopping, returns to the parking lot, where a dark man lurks around the parked cars. In terror she flees back into the supermarket.* In this dream the dreamer's Demeter-like activity, food gathering, constellates the Underworld (dark) rapist. In defense, she flees back into the supermarket (amongst the thousand-and-one daily things). That is, her Demeter qualities now turn into a defense against the rape.

(2) *The dreamer, a young woman, is walking home alone after a Transcendental Meditation meeting, when she realizes a man is following her. She rushes into the nearest house and then later realizes that the man of the house is actually the rapist. She awakes in terror.* For this dreamer, her transcendental activities have the effect of calming her and holding dark forces in abeyance. But this time, as she leaves the meeting, the counter-threat of dark attack immediately appears. She flees into the nearest, apparently civilized (Demeter and Hera) structure, but finds that even this (which had once been collective safety) is now the home of the rapist, the house of Hades himself. For this dreamer there would seem no way out but finally to submit to the initiation of the dark forces –whatever they might be.

(3) *The dreamer is in a disco when a hand from beneath the table reaches up her leg. She smashes her glass against the hand and spills the liquor.* In this dream, at least the dreamer's container of spirits was broken, giving the possibility of a deeper, Underworld containment. But the action is a token defense, appearing in many areas of her life. She was continually "breaking her glass," so that "spirits" flowed everywhere, in a repetitive effort to ward off the hand beneath the table.

More often, however, in rape dreams the dreamer appears to flee entirely the Persephone/Demeter constellation and turns instead to another: fleeing toward the light, calling the police, rushing to her husband, locking the car doors, etc. The variety and desperateness of the defense to rape situations attest to just how unbearable this archetypal constellation is for collective consciousness. [41] It is not that these situations cannot also be reflected from the Demeter/Persephone perspective. Rather, it is that these moves become attempts to get out altogether from this archetypal pattern and the necessity of its rape.

Much more fashionable nowadays is holding one's ground, standing for one's rights – all of which is understandable in the light of contemporary events. But the accompanying difficulty is that by pushing ourselves forward as subjects we then lose touch with the possibility of experiencing ourselves back and downwards as objects. [42] We forget that to be raped into consciousness is also a way.

Even if the occasion of psychic rape is not foreign to us, we haven't known where to put it. And so we have had to fight off the experience all the more blindly. A working archetypal model for these overpowering, backward, downward movements is given by the Demeter/Persephone myth, in which rape was after all elevated to the status of a mystery

41 Cf. Jung, *Science of Mythology* ([above, n. 17], 160), where he points out the modern prejudice against Underworld – chthonic material.

42 Jung (ibid., 156) views the "Kore" as the self and the *anima*. He also states that both self and *anima* tend to be experienced as objects rather than as subjects (161). If we take all of this internally, it is likely that in the experience of ourselves as objects (rather than as ego subjects), there is also the possibility of experience in greater depth (what Jung calls the self).

in ancient Greece. [43] Because we have lost these rites, rape is now even more threatening, and therefore we have a great deal of difficulty experiencing Demeter/Persephone consciousness in any but the most superficial, defensive, and neurotic ways. In order to deepen this archetypal consciousness, a more trenchant and effective analysis of our Demeter defenses is needed. Beyond this analysis and ultimately, however, it is perhaps only our love for the daughter, and therefore for the Underworld, the *telos* of our symptoms, that makes certain our movement down and into depth.

---

43 When speaking of the Eleusinian mysteries (whose initiates were men as well as women), Kerényi (*Science of Mythology* ([above, n. 17], 139) says: "The passivity of Persephone, of the bride, the maiden doomed to die, is re-experienced by means of an inner act – if only an act of surrender." For an in-depth study on the Eleusinian mysteries, see his *Eleusis* (above, n. 19).

III

The Dogma of Gender

When depth psychology speaks of its fantasies of early childhood, certain consistent features stand out: the variety of sexual forms. There are oral things, anal things, genital things – each of which gives pleasure in its own way. Psychology's fantasy of childhood says that we are many-sexed and that there are many forms in which our sexuality is expressed. Moreover, all of these pleasures are nongender pleasures. Gender identification doesn't come until later. Before settling as little males and little females, we are polymorphously perverse, kinky, and sexy all over; every part of the body is involved, at some time or other, in one or another form of eroticism.

Let me quote from Freud some of the characteristics of the sexual instincts: "They are numerous, emanate from manifold organic sources, act... independently of one another and only at a late stage achieve a more or less complete synthesis. The aim which each strives to attain is 'organ-pleasure'... "[44] "... they have in a high degree the capacity to act vicariously for one another and... can readily change their objects."[45] The sexual instinct has the strange capacity of being able to reverse into its opposite – from passive to active, from active to passive.[46]

---

44 S. Freud, "Instincts and their Vicissitudes," in *Collected Papers*, vol. 4 (London: Hogarth Press, 1925), 68.
45 Ibid., 69.
46 Ibid.

Whether Freud is "right" about infantile sexuality is not the question here. I am concerned only with his fantasy. To summarize this fantasy:

(1) Childhood sexuality is inferior, lower, and not of our better selves. It is shameful from the perspective of more mature faculties.

(2) These instincts were originally various and numerous and came from manifold sources. Their aim was unity, synthesis. That is, if we managed to get it all together, then we have become one, a unit, and either a male or female unit.

(3) Pre-gender sexuality is something past. Manifold and numerous sexuality was true of us once, but – heaven knows – not now. It was something pre-, before the healthy, fully developed persons we now are.

(4) These instincts were organic: they came from the body, are in the body. (So in later life one way to rid ourselves of these instincts is to reject the body.)

(5) Their aim was pleasure: simply physical, organ pleasure, having nothing to do at their origin with reproduction, which requires genders.

(6) They are ambivalent, changeable, becoming first this, then that. You cannot pin them down. Active becomes passive and passive turns active.

To develop out of this pleasurable, polymorphous, childish, multiple, perverse, inferior, confused state as quickly and completely as possible is the psychoanalytic aim. But now, having safely accomplished this heroic feat of maturing, let us make the reverse movement. Just for fun, let us put our maturity aside and return to that projected fantasy state, that pre-gender condition called infantile childhood.

There are some disadvantages in this return. For one, it may make us feel ashamed and inadequate. Beware of anyone who says he does not feel at least uncomfortable back there. Not to feel lowly the polymorphous realm denies part of the experience, that fantasy of the polymorphous as inferior, confused, lower, inadequate, nonproductive. If we take seriously the phenomena of our fantasy, *we cannot have the pleasurable vicissitudes of sexual instinct without this sense of inferiority*. In fact, the inferiority is one of the instinct's very vicissitudes, part of its very pleasure. So let us keep the pleasure and inferiority together, not split into lust and guilt, Id and Superego.

Here, I would like to remind you of Euripides' *The Bacchae*. The play begins as Dionysus arrives in Thebes to teach his rites, which he does with a vengeance since the people of Thebes have not recognized his divinity. To correct this omission, Dionysus incites the women of the town to a wild religious frenzy; they rush from their households and take to the hills in Bacchic celebration.

Pentheus, the ruler of Thebes, is enraged by this Bacchic madness yet also secretly fascinated. He does not, however, join in, but, rather, climbs a tree over the site of the revelry to watch. He revels in looking down on it all from above. Eventually the unconscious libido, these dancing, libidinous maenads, turn on him – they don't like being looked down on – and one of them, Agave, Pentheus's own mother, tears him to shreds.

This kind of superego superiority (in Freud's terms), or one-sided attitude split from the unconscious (in Jung's), is bound to result in wild revenge from the primal, the mother. The more Pentheus sets himself apart from and superior to maenad forces, the more dangerous the situation; the more polarized, the more explosive. And besides, who's kinky really – the many who are dancing or the one high up in the tree?

But just to *be* these primal forces, the maenads, is not the point either, because that self-indulgence is precisely what sends Pentheus up a tree – call him superego, parents, authorities, society, legislation.

Wild expression and upper repression need and seem to constellate each other. The moment we lose ourselves in one, the other is going to occur. So it is crucial to step aside from this maenad-versus-Pentheus structure, identifying neither with the fantasy of full, wild expression nor the fantasy of safe superiority.

Fortunately there is a built-in safeguard to keep us from this polarized situation, a safeguard belonging to the primal zone itself. We are protected from within it by a sense of weakness, the inferiority that we mentioned as accompanying the experience of the primal level. So long as we feel sensitive about hungry mouths, anus, clitoris, penis, about bowels and masturbation, they will not appear as overwhelming powers.

When we are in touch with them, we will also be in touch with a sense of inferiority. Where there is primal sexuality, there is at the same time inhibiting humility.

Of course, there are many ways around this humility, many ways to deny it. I might say I would not feel so inferior and inhibited in these lower regions if my mother had not done such or my father been so. These rationalizations (like all rationalizations) keep me unconscious. I can remain childlike and powerful by pretending that my family circumstances were just an "accident" that got in the way of my natural self. I'd be okay were it not for others. There is an omnipotence fantasy, a hidden inflation, in this urge to blame my problems on parents and surroundings – as though out of any context, unsullied by the world, I would have been without inferiority or ambiguity.

An Eastern idea puts it the other way round. According to this view, each soul is born into the precise family and circumstances necessary for its individuation. My soul chose my family as just what it needed. My mother and father are precisely the sort my psyche required for its fate. The shock of this thought shows how much we have invested in external determinism and how dedicated we are to disowning natal realities. Actually the two experiences go together, external causation and internal inflation.

So let us consider the sense of instinctual erogenous inferiority as autochthonous and basic to the primal zone itself. Let us affirm that to be pre-gender or nongender is also to feel inferior.

Inferiority was stressed by another depth psychologist, Alfred Adler. He spoke of organ inferiority, by which he meant an inferiority rooted in the physical body. As Freud's fantasy was bodily, so, too, was Adler's. But by imagining an actual organ as afflicted, Adler evoked a more literal, biological sense of infirmity, infirmity as the basis of physical being.

What was Adler getting at with this idea? In Freud's view, one could grow out of much of one's polymorphous perversity, leaving only a few traces (as foreplay). But Adler insisted we do not grow out of these inferiorities so much as construct opposites to delude ourselves away from them. The basic pair of these dichotomized opposites for Adler is masculine and feminine. In other words, *the construct of gender protects us from feeling our inferiority.*

The neurotic then orients his life according to these opposites of masculine-feminine and goes on to collect, with some help from the culture, more opposites along the same lines. Masculine-feminine becomes brave-cowardly, rich-poor, cruel-tender, victorious-defeated, defiant-obedient, and so on.

By entering into masculine and feminine constructs, we move into the neurosis that has been built to compensate the inferiority we feel in infancy as organic, physical beings. Since we need to do something with this inferiority, we construct opposite poles, one from which to flee and one toward which to strive. Of course, the "feminine" is that from which to flee and the "masculine" that toward which to strive.

Do note here that it is not only we women who are cursed with this experience of inferiority. Men are too. We all have a kind of penis envy, a castration anxiety, and feeling of biological inadequacy. We all strive away from pre-gender consciousness, what Adler called "psychic hermaphroditism," and then spend our lives trying to compensate this basic sense of inferiority. Unfortunately, in the flight from inferiority we lose the pleasure as well.

*

But gender, too, brings pleasure – a pleasure of another kind, one that has to do precisely with male and female, the play between them, their tensions and unions. Gender cannot be ignored.

Ideas of gender distinction, of masculine and feminine, exist the world over and are utilized by most cultures in their languages, social structures, and mythologies. Gender is archetypal. We have always thought in terms of gender, and most probably some part of us always will. But that doesn't mean we need think that way all the time.

That gender is a form in which we *can* feel and think and experience does not make it right or true. If it is archetypal, it requires exactly that we *not* think this way all the time. For if we take one archetypal perspective exclusively, we are caught by it. And the result of being caught by an archetype is that experience shrinks. We cannot see beyond the archetype's confines, and we begin to interpret more and more of our experience only in its terms. We get single-minded. An archetypal idea *per se* is an overvalued idea that must be "seen through" and placed in perspective.

But still, and once again, this gender archetype is so especially pleasurable! In fact, I wonder if pleasure is not precisely what gender is about. When thinking and seeing in terms of gender, are we not engaging in a pleasurable way of perceiving – a way that eroticizes and engenders, brings to life, the world around us?

The difference between pre-gender pleasure and the pleasure of gender may simply be that we feel the first (pre-gender) as primitive, inferior, multiple, narcissistic and low, that is, "bad" pleasure. While the second, blessed by society and by psychology, we feel as mature, reality-oriented, related, productive, that is, "good" pleasure, which is also ego-syntonic. And here again is the rub: ego-syntonic tends to become ego-defensive. What agrees with the ego supports and is used by it. Thus begins the dogma of gender.

*

Thanks to the women's movement, most of us are aware of the pervasiveness of sexism in our culture. Perhaps it is time to look to ourselves to see what sorts of gender thinking we, too, have engaged in. There are two strands within feminist thinking that, for the sake of imaginative simplification, I will treat as though they were two distinct characters. But bear in mind that my subject is gender thinking and not feminist thinking. I am inventing these imaginative simplifications not to criticize actual women or feminism, but to look more closely into dogmatic ways of thinking that would distort the intentions of feminism by exclusively and defensively identifying it with gender.

The first character says: "I am a woman – biologically, emotionally, in my very being. Because I am a woman, my values are different from those of men. It is unnatural for me to think hierarchically or analytically. Society, because it is the result of men's thinking, oppresses my femininity. I want more attention paid to Women's needs: daycare centers, wages for my housework, more adequate divorce laws. Furthermore,

I want women in government and in the boardroom. Being women, they will bring a feminine eros and understanding to offset male rationality. I want women, that is, 'the feminine,' to be more highly valued."

A second strand of feminism or feminist caricature says: "Don't tell me what it is to be a woman. Don't talk to me of 'the feminine.' Femininity is a category invented by men to keep women inferior and pliable, fulfilling men's needs. Don't tell me my duty is to feel, receive, bring eros or beauty. I shall bring whatever I, as an individual, bring. I am first of all a person, and I want nothing barred from me on the basis of gender. I can think analytically and work creatively. Moreover, I can climb telephone poles, drive trucks, build houses, and do road work. My body is my own to do with as I wish, sexually or otherwise, and I shall dress and walk and talk however I choose."

It is not a question of siding with one or the other of these carica-tures. From a psychological point of view, either may be using her ideas of gender defensively. Let's take the first: her idea of femininity, her gender, is her ego identity. She knows what she knows *because* she is a woman. Because she is a woman, she thinks differently and has access to feelings that men, because they are men, lack.

This collective attitude we all share to the extent that we think in terms of male propensities and female propensities. The problem comes when we organize expectations around these assumptions. For example, in many Jungian training institutes, trainees are required to analyze with both a female and a male analyst, the idea being that these experiences will complement one another. With a woman analyst, the experience will be more feeling, more motherly and receptive with greater emphasis on "eros." With a male, it will be harder, more phallic and "*logos*"-oriented. This notion of analysis presupposes all sorts of gender principles and assumes that analyzed persons act in accord with mature gender-identified characteristics.

Gender may be used to justify personality traits. When I explain be-havior on the basis of gender – "I do this *because* I am a woman" – I gain an identity and self-affirmation that is difficult to question. There is no doubt about physical gender, so when my attitudes are tied to and buttressed by this referent, they, too, may not be doubted. Engendered attitudes are self-containing and self-confirming. Because our female bodies are internal, receiving and sensitive, we are superior in internality, feelings and sensitivities – simply *because* we are women.

This gender-identified attitude deters the deeper intentions of feminism, for it turns the richness of individual self-discovery into a sexism that narrows rather than broadens perception and experience. That is to say, the person who sees through these defensive gender spectacles may come to see only in terms of them.

I know someone who perceives even countries and nationalities as masculine or feminine. Southern countries are feminine since they inspire feeling, eros, and body. Northern countries are masculine because they are cold and evoke thinking, spirit, intellect. Any Italian, Greek, or Spaniard in a dream automatically means eros whereas an Englishman or Scandinavian is thinking and intellectual, regardless of who the particular figure is and what he or she is doing in the dream. Even animals are "gendered." Cats and water birds and boa constrictors are female; lions, dogs, and horses male, as though animals came in only one sex. The specific image or individual in the dream is clouded in the easy generality of gender. Dogma in psychology exists frequently where we are most fuzzy, not necessarily where our attitudes are sharp and unyielding.

Of course, the situation is worse when a male or female figure in a dream is acting in a contra- or nongendered way. Should a male figure be, say, knitting, and a female performing a surgical operation – then the figures have most certainly gone wrong. To those who look at it this way, it is never our gender *ideas* that are in need of reshaping, but, rather, dream *figures* that continue to be not as they ought. Such is the power of dogma.

Dogmas bar us from perceptive and particularized feeling as they truncate original, interesting thought. Wearing these simple gender blinders, we write whole books in terms of masculine (patriarchy) and feminine (matriarchy), interpret whole epochs, entire lives.

I mentioned a second strand of feminism or feminist character, the one at war with gender distinction of any sort. She, too, may use her gender ideas defensively. Whereas the first figure made an ego identity of her femininity, thereby bolstering herself, the second, feeling her biological gender to be a weakness, assumes her strength lies elsewhere. When she is feminine, she cannot be strong; when she is strong, she cannot be feminine. This character seeks to prove herself, so she takes on tasks that require great physical and/or emotional strength. Or – and this is more frequent – she performs her work *as though* it required great strength, making the effort, not the results, her confirmation. She is "strong" because she is driven to do things in a strong way.

This character, also, has identified the qualities of softness, receptiveness, relatedness, and eros with femininity. But because she is not the sort to gather power through these qualities, she defines her ego in contrast to them.

*

We have looked at two kinds of gender thinking, each dogmatic and defensive. We have also, however, recognized gender as a pleasurable biological and social fact. So the question: how might we enjoy the delight of gender without falling into these defensive, limiting dogmas?

One move might be to reconnect gender with the original pre-gender realm of pleasure. Rather than viewing gender as a development away from the polymorphous, perhaps we may experience it as another form of the many pleasures – one of the ways sensuality enjoys itself.

This shift of emphasis, though slight, dethrones gender from its sovereign claim to unity and superiority, unseats it from its pinnacle the most highly developed and unquestioned state. Perhaps it is not gender as such that is the problem anyway, but its singleness, the monotheism of gender, gender as the epitome of unity and identity.

When gender is restored to its polymorphous roots in pleasure, rejoined with an awareness of variety, changeability, shifts of role and function – then its pleasure includes a sense of the lower, the multiple and the incomplete. Gender sexuality by claiming less enjoys itself more, freed from the self-justifying, defensive dogmas surrounding it.

Experienced as polymorphous, gender becomes a quality of particulars rather than a generality into which particulars must fit. Sexual details – a male shape of buttock, a female curve of hip – become qualities adding to the individual, in the same way as do height, eye color, body build, and other sensuous particulars.

Roughness and softness, squares and curves, subtle movements of penetrating and receiving bring pleasure to a life experienced immediately, variously, and complexly. As a painter would not begin a portrait with a generality, neither would a sensuous experience of life begin with an overall scheme as to how life ought to be. Yet the idea of gender does precisely that.

Often those who have most notably viewed the world in terms of gender distinction, from the pre-Socratics through Aristotle and on, were concerned primarily with thought. Their task was to form concepts, build classifications and organizational schemes. Linnaeus, for example, used gender to order the botanical world. Freud schematized the meaning of symbols in terms of gender morphology. We draw upon gender distinctions when we need the broadest possible conceptual organization. Yin/Yang, lunar/solar, right/left brain, passive/active, matriarchy/patriarchy provide large oppositional categories. Biological gender is usually clearly observable, universal, unambiguous, offering a point of view that need not be confused by the variety and ambivalence of phenomena. This gender simplicity works for more than biology. I find that when I am confused, exasperated, or overwhelmed with emotion, I fall back on basic and unambiguous ways of organizing. I say, "Why does he always do that? Because he's a man – that's why!" I explain on the basis of gender something that would take more differentiation than I have available at the moment.

But most of the time one does not need these rough-and-ready categories. Usually one is free to enjoy perceiving persons as they are, each in a style of individual complexity. Then gender categories and schemes are an interference. When attributes are organized and taped, one can't hear, can't see, can't sense apart from the terms already given. Besides, a good deal of individuality is pre-gender.

*

The two caricatures we looked at earlier were "straight" in their relations to gender. By straight I mean their notions of gender were unambiguous. Each in her manner – one by being female, the other anti-female – had ironed out the kinks in her identification. Each had limited her awareness to a narrow ego realm in which she felt adequacy and power. Put aside were the many forms and inferior feelings of the polymorphous.

This straightening occurs in many other ways as well. In the field of psychology, it appears especially in what we call *identity*. A few years ago, the Trustees of the American Psychiatric Association announced they would no longer consider homosexuality a mental disorder. But what *was* a disorder, they maintained, was "sexual orientation disturbances." This means that someone who believes herself homosexual and lives as a homosexual with no qualms is okay. The moment she wavers, the moment she thinks, "I don't know. Sometimes I feel maybe something else, I don't know…" – well, then she is sick. Or he, of course.

In other words, what the American Psychiatric Association is after is straightness – and it no longer matters whether heterosexual or homosexual. It doesn't matter which way one is straight, just so all kinks are made smooth, just so the person has identified completely and unambiguously.

Yet, on its deepest level, where sexuality touches the basis of being, does it not bring up unexpected contradictions, surprising moments, peculiar feelings? Are we not all at times rather confused concerning sexuality – where it is coming from, what it wants, where it has gone? To straighten all this out would be to miss it. Sexuality *is* the unexpected. Through it, consciousness drops into deeper bodily and more mysterious grounds.

Going straight also hurts marriage – an institution that anyway has that tendency in its legal and social functions. Couples often report that though they enjoyed their sex life before, now that they are married, the fun has disappeared. One woman said that many of the sexual pleasures she enjoyed before marriage she now no longer dared enjoy. It was somehow too embarrassing. By taking the straight vows of marriage with its gender roles, she had straightened out as well her subsocial, polymorphous possibilities.

It difficult to bring the perverse levels of the psyche into marriage. To do so is a *contra-naturam* act, demanding effort and attention. The most natural, easiest, and unobstructed course is to follow the flow simply into marital straightness (and eventually marital boredom).

Even the current notion of androgyny presents an opportunity for straightening. Here again, the idea of opposites is drawn upon (there are masculine qualities and feminine ones), but with androgyny they are imagined to be carefully proportioned. With our "masculine" qualities and our "feminine" qualities balanced, we are safe from psychological extremities.

What the concept of androgyny declares as really truly masculine and genuinely feminine ends up in a realm of concepts and abstractions: plus and minus systems, circles, Venus and Mars, a "human" figure neatly drawn and perfectly divided. Missing is any sense of flesh, pain, confusion, or even life. The very word *androgyny* is clinically clean, straight, and sterile, free from the germs of time and struggle and disrepute. There is no sense of inferiority, for androgyny is the transcending, transsexual solution, not the soiling one.

A curious fact about psychological work is that it requires dirty words. Patients use dirty words. Words rank, tangled, conflicted, and smelling of history are humus for the soul in its struggles. To lose this dirt in the language of the psyche leaves the soil of the psyche barren.

The real difference between androgyny and polymorphousness is the experience. Let us imagine that I experience myself as an androgyne, a little bit masculine here, a little feminine there. I feel okay, balanced into an idealized construct about myself.

The reason I prefer to experience myself as a bit soiled and kinky is that it preserves my primal, historical sense. If those experiences of dirtiness and inadequacy were as important in the formation of my particular personality as depth psychology claims they were, then if I value myself and my uniqueness, that basis is sacred. The basis is base and the bottom soiled.

Of course, *anything* can turn into a defense. One can ride one's inadequacy as a masochism; one can become genderless in a sexless, childish way. But again, by becoming identified – with the child in this case – one has become straight. Indeed *any move can become straight and defensive.* Any move can become an identification – straight child, straight male, straight female, straight androgyne.

★

With the resolve not to identify in any of these ways, let us return to the pleasure principle, which for Freud rules the polymorphous realm. This principle is the desire for immediate gratification.

Yet it is strange how pleasures wear themselves out. Something pleasurable at one moment is no longer so at the next. Pleasures grow weary of themselves and then seek new refinements in order to become again enjoyable.

Half the world was discovered due to pleasure's drive for refinement. What made us think we needed silk, damask, muslin, satin, velvet; sugar, pepper, ginger, cloves, cinnamon; maize, sesame, rice, lemons, melons, peaches, apricots, cherries, dates...? What made us tire of our simple meads, driving us to the many refinements of drink? What bored us with our daily bread, our basic meat, to develop the variety and complexity of cooking we have today? (Certainly it was no notion of balanced vitamins and minerals.) What moves our continual changes in fashion and in decoration, our explorations in architecture, literature, painting, music? Indeed, our very culture is testament to some mad, autonomous drive within pleasure for its own refinement.

Add to this the enormous variety of different kinds of pleasure – the oral pleasures: subtleties of taste, texture, heat, smell, the fact that this with that tastes different from this with something else; the anal pleasures: work, discipline, putting aside, holding back and cutting off, building up, emotion, color, tension; letting it all out, exploding, making, creating, defining. To differentiate in the realm of pleasure we need never climb out and look down wisely from above. Pleasure has in itself its own differentiation, and in fact pleasure *demands* it.

The polymorphous underrealm has form and *logos* within it. As the pseudo-Democritus is said to have said that "nature rejoices in nature, nature subdues nature, and nature rules over nature."[47] We might say the same concerning nature's pleasure: pleasure rejoices in pleasure, pleasure subdues pleasure, and pleasure rules over pleasure. The poly-

---

47 C.G. Jung, *Mysterium Coniunctionis*, Collected Works, trans. R.F.C. Hull, vol. 14 (Princeton Univ. Press, 1970), 152n.

morphous realm continuously works on itself – defining, refining, and recombining its pleasures.

This work within pleasure upon pleasure implies a kind of natural light, *lumen naturalis*. As we end, let me relate a dream of a young woman in which this appears:

> Her sister (whom she regards as fat, stupid and ordinary – the one who stays at home) is pulling her by the foot deeper and deeper down in the ocean. She struggles, but finally gives in to her sister's downward pull. As she descends she finds to her surprise that there is air in the depths. She can breathe. The region is infused with a natural, phosphorescent light emanating from shapes in the depths.

In the deepest regions beneath the ocean, nature reveals its own light. This lower, instinctual, many-formed level of our biological existence has light and is highly organized – like the dance of the maenads (and not at all the dark and wildly chaotic force we sometimes project it as being).

When we experience this pre-gender realm as dark and chaotic – when we feel that if we let go of gender identification and ideas of masculine and feminine, if we let perversity into awareness and other sexual forms into society, then indeed everything will break down – we are within a particular archetypal constellation, and it may happen according to how we prophesy it.

When we feel this way, we might stop and see where we are looking from. Most probably we are balanced high up in a tree, like Pentheus, superior to it all, looking down.

DREAM

IV

An Approach to the Dream

> But every psychic process, so far as it can be observed as
> such, is essentially *theoria*, that is to say, it is a *presentation;*
> and its reconstruction – or "re-presentation" – is at best
> only a variant of the same presentation. [48]
> – C. G. Jung

Once upon a time a Jungian analysand appeared strangely distraught. It seems she had had occasion to show someone else a dream she and her analyst had worked on in a previous session, and then was so unsettled with the disparity of interpretation that she had rushed off for a third and then a fourth opinion – all differed essentially. Dream interpretation, she now charged, was a pseudo-science and interpreters mere charlatans.

Although this parable can reflect a number of problems about analysis, and this sort of analysand in particular, it also gives cause for some theoretical reflection about dreams. Of course, any dream has a variety of possible interpretations; of course, each analyst has his particular biases, approaches, and assumptions. But still, aren't some interpretations more to the point somehow than others? Let's take a look at her dream:

---

48 "Analytical Psychology and Education: Three Lectures," in *Development of Personality*, Collected Works, trans. R. F. C. Hull, vol. 17 (Princeton Univ. Press, 1970), par. 162.

> I was lying on a bed in a room, alone apparently, but with the feel-
> ing of turmoil around me. A middle-aged woman enters and hands
> me a key. Later a man enters, helps me out of bed, and leads me
> upstairs to an unknown room.

We may imagine a variety of Jungian analysts and the sort of interpretation each might give for this dream:

(1) *Ego-active analyst:* The whole dream is characterized by your ego
passivity. You are reclining, a rather unconscious position, which makes
for the feeling of unconscious turmoil. Without effort of your own, you
take what is handed to you. You are led away by the *animus*, therefore, up
into yet another area of passive fantasy.

(2) *Relationship-feeling analyst:* You're alone in a room, isolated, and
cut off from your marriage, relationships, children. Never do you express feeling for or make any real contact with the other figures in the
dream. Therefore, you are led into the upper regions with only your *animus* as companion, alone and remote, the princess in the tower.

(3) *Transference-oriented analyst:* You're in a half-conscious sexual position, in which the turmoil represents your unrecognized erotic projections. You fantasy various solutions: a) the phallic mother, or b) the man
leading you upstairs to an unknown climax. One of these (depending
upon sex) refers to your projection of me as your savior.

(4) *Animus-development analyst:* When you confront your turmoil, it becomes the middle-aged woman, your fear of growing old and unfruitful.
But in that older woman you find the creative key that becomes then the
unknown *animus* who leads you to the higher room, that is, to the unknown part of your psyche in which creative work can now take place.

(5) *Introvert analyst:* There you are at last alone with yourself, in the
vessel. You receive now inner help. Your inner femininity gives you the
key, the key being seclusion and facing the internal turmoil hitherto denied by your extraverted defenses and acting out. This leads you to the
next step, the *animus* figure who helps you out of bed and leads you to
another level.

(6) *Feminine Earth-Mother analyst:* You were lying passive, naturally, in
touch with your real feelings (depressive position). Now you can receive

gifts from the feminine, the positive mother. Unfortunately, as soon as the *animus* appears, you lose this connection by following him up into the intellect.

(7) *Process-oriented analyst:* It's not so much the content of the dream as the way you have introduced it into our session (that you told it to me in such an aggressive voice, that you waited until the end of the hour, that you handed it to me neatly typed and then leaned back passively waiting for an interpretation).

As we read these seven statements, how glaring the analyst's assumptions seem in some of them and how true or accurate in others. Yet any one of these perspectives could be derived from Jung's writings on the dream, and none of them is necessarily wrong. We are not here concerned with "right" or "wrong" in regard to the above responses – rather why it is that we prefer one over another. We can avoid the problem by saying it all depends upon the patient's reaction – which interpretation "clicks" for him. But however practical this approach, it conceals an essential difficulty having to do with what might be called theoretical sensitivity.

We know from the comparative studies that have been done on theoretical schools and styles of therapy that virtually every therapy works. Every therapy shows evidence of accomplishing the aims it sets for itself, and all fail to the same extent. Though not in itself surprising, the relativism of therapy in terms of results can lead to frightening consequences. It opens the way to an aspect of psychotherapy little different from charlatanism, syntonic transference neurosis, hysterical suggestion, doctrinal compliance, religious conversion, and political brainwashing. For these, too, "click," and in these, too, the subject feels himself changed for the better on the basis insights revealed. Without a sensitivity among theories, it no longer matters what theory we have; one idea is as good as another, providing it works – and everything works equally. If there are better and worse theories about dream interpretation, they cannot be based on what "clicks" – for when we lose sensitivity here, we lose it in practice as well.

Furthermore, since our main mode of reflecting about what we are doing is by means of dreams, it is here of all places that becoming aware of our assumptions is of fundamental importance. It is the crux of our practice. The alchemists did not only perform experiments, they spent their time equally in a kind of *theoria* – *praying*, reading, and thinking in relation to what they were doing. In fact, to make practicality our determinant criterion is a kind of immorality, the sort we also see in the psychopath who says what works is therefore good. But rather than get too carried away with this charge against the moral cop-out of pragmatism, perhaps it would be more advantageous to turn to its contrary, the psychological importance of theory.

Because theory so determines practice – after all what we practice is theory – in order to be aware of what we're doing with dreams, we have to become aware of what we're thinking about dreams. We have to examine not only how we put our theory into practice, but also what we are putting into practice. This means turning to our assumptions and becoming aware of our unconsciousness in this realm too.

So what we will be elaborating in this paper is a tool (one among many) for more precisely grasping our underlying ideas when we look at dreams. Our intention is to work out some means for *interpretative self-awareness*, a method by which we may examine our actual interpretative process, interpret our own interpretations.

As we have maintained, methods have underlying assumptions, so this method, too, implies a theoretical position. Our basic premise is that the dream is something in and of itself. It is an imaginal product in its own right. Regardless of what we do or don't do with it, it is an image.

1. *Image*

> We must stick to the Image!
> – Rafael López-Pedraza

Following Jung, by image we "do not mean the psychic reflection of an external object, but a concept derived from poetic usage, namely, a figure of fancy or *fantasy-image*."[49] In this passage, Jung gives ground for a

---

49 C. G. Jung, *Psychological Types*, Collected Works, trans. R. F. C. Hull, vol. 6 (Princeton Univ. Press, 1971), par. 743.

distinction between imagination and perception. A fantasy-image is sensate though not perceptual: i.e., it has obvious sensual qualities – form, color, texture – but these are not derived from external objects. On the other hand, perception has to do with objective reals – what I see is real and there. And so, by claiming external reality, hallucinations (psychotic or psychedelic) pertain to perception, whereas dream images pertain to imagination. The two modes, imaginal and perceptual, rely upon distinctly different psychic functions. With imagination any question of objective referent is irrelevant. The imaginal is quite real in its own way, but never *because* it corresponds to something outer. Though dream figures and places frequently borrow the visage of perceptual reality, they need not be derived from perception. As we read from Jung, images in our dreams are not reflections of external objects, but are "inner images."

But why then, it may be asked, do we sometimes dream of figures from our perceptual world and at other times of figures never perceived? Certainly, the familiar figure must be some sort of afterimage or *Tagesrest*. The traditional manner in which we deal with images that correspond with perceptual figures is to call them products of the personal unconscious and then seek to sort out the projections they carry for us. So far so good, for it seems what we're really doing is attempting to redeem these images from their perceptual imprisonment and to reclaim them as psychic, thereby shifting our standpoint from perceptual to imaginal.

But this cannot take place, our exit from this perceptual world becomes blocked, our movement stuck, when we deal with these so-called personal figures on a personal level, forgetting that they are fundamentally fantasy-images cloaked in after-images. Personal figures are precisely those most bound to our literal perspective. When my spouse, children, or friend appear in my dream, they have become to some extent removed from the "reality" of the perceptual world with which they are so closely associated. The dream offers the opportunity to make metaphorical these figures, and thus the psyche may be seen as working *toward* the imaginal, away from the perceptual – repetitively and insistently. This movement may be regarded as the psyche's *opus contra naturam*, a work away from the natural reality of the perceptual toward the psychic reality of the imaginal.

Now we must look more closely at the kind of reality an image has. We have to examine with more exactitude just what we mean here by an image, and one of these ways is to take it apart, performing a kind of *analysis of the image.*

Sensuality: One reason why images so easily merge with the after-images of sense perception is that images, too, are sensate; images, too, imply a body of sorts. But this body is no more a perceptual "natural" body than are images derived from perceptual natural objects. The body to which images refer is metaphorical, a psychic body in which the sensory combinations and all the sense qualities of the image that would for perception be outlandish, incomplete, overwhelming, or distorted in some respect or other, here make sense.

Texture: The word *text* is related to weave. So to be faithful to a text is to feel and follow its weave. When we speak of putting a dream in its context, meaning with the text of the dreamer's life, we tend to neglect that the dream is sensate, has texture, is woven with patterns offering a finished and full context. The life situation need not be the only means by which to connect the dream with this textural aspect. Image in itself has texture.

Emotion: Also inseparable from both sensuality and texture is emotion. A dream image is or has a quality of emotion. Dream moments may be expansive, oppressive, empty, menacing, excited... These emotional qualities are not necessarily portrayed verbally by the dreamer in his report, by the dream ego in his reactions, or by other figures in the dream. They adhere or inhere to the image and may not be explicit at all. Even if unrecognized by the dreamer in the dream, they are crucial for connecting with the images. We cannot entertain any image in dreams, or poetry, or painting without experiencing an emotional quality presented by the image itself.

Simultaneity: An image is simultaneous. No part precedes or causes another part, although all parts are involved with each other. So we view the image level of the dream as nonprogressive; no part occurs before or leads to any other part. We might image the dream as a series of superimpositions, each event adding texture and thickening to the rest. In the dream above we might then say that the horizontal dream ego, the woman with the key, and the man leading upstairs are all expressions essential to the psychic state; none carries a secondary meaning. They are all layers of each other and inseparable in time. Such relationship we might express as *while* or *when*. While the dream ego is lying alone in turmoil, a middle-aged woman hands a key and a man leads to an unknown room. It does not matter which phrase comes "first" because there can be no priority in an image – all is given at once. Everything is occurring *while* everything else is occurring, in different ways, simultaneously. Jung's emphasis upon the "present situation" need not be identified with the literal life situation, which removes the dream from the presence of the image, but also might be read to mean that every part of the dream is concurrently present.

Intrarelations: All the elements (characters, settings, situations) within a dream are in some sense connected. They are each part of the overall dream image, so that no part can be selected out, or pitted against the other parts. By this complete intrarelation of the dream we mean to point out the full democracy of the image: that all parts have an equal right to be heard and belong to the body politic, and that there are no privileged positions within the image. (This is not to deny the innate hierarchies within the image, which we shall come to below under *Value.*) Let's look at an example showing how intrarelatedness appears in a dream image. A woman dreamed:

> I am in bed when a funny little dwarf emerges from beneath the covers. He is shyly glancing at me as though he wants some sexual contact. Just at that moment my friend R. (a conservative, responsible, older man) appears at the door and urgently shouts, "Run!" as though I am in some great danger.

One way of viewing this dream would be to take the conservative friend R. and the tricky little dwarf as opposites between which the dreamer must choose. But this approach would be to *fix* them into opposition, to reinforce what is already the dream ego's experience. By taking into account the coincidence of the opposites (the *coincidental oppositorum*), which is to say the total dream image in which all parts fit, however, we would see the panicked R. as actually constellated by the amorous dwarf, and vice versa. The two of them together *are* the image. In daily life, when the dreamer is connected to her dwarf creativity, trickiness, and so forth, her conservative, responsible *animus* panics and urges her to run, to cut herself off from the dwarflike, lower aspects; and hence, the other way round, when the responsible *animus* is in a state of panic, somewhere, probably very unconsciously, an assignation with the dwarf is occurring. In daily life, she drops her purse, loses her keys, unconsciously creates misunderstanding... If we are to stick to this imagistic level of the dream, the point is to refrain from choosing between characters.

Frequently we must also hold a tension within settings. A man dreamed:

> I walked into my mother's kitchen and saw an Encyclopedia Britannica on the counter.

The image is his mother's kitchen within which is an encyclopedia. An immediate tendency would be to destroy this image by saying, for example, an encyclopedia doesn't belong in a kitchen, or that just shows his mother's *animus*. Whereas the former would be to betray the image altogether (for the most effective images do, in fact, conjoin the most unfitting opposites), the latter would be in itself an *animus* statement – a preconceived judgment. But by giving the image the recognition and dignity of a psychic product infinitely more profound than we, we may find ourselves stilled. Within his mother's kitchen is an encyclopedia, or a toad, or a maimed old man. Already the psyche has done something, something is happening in his mother's kitchen. For him the point is to work on this image (and let this image work on him) in whatever imaginative/experiential ways he can – which requires holding in abeyance his judgment and interpretation.

Value: Some images seem more potent, more highly attractive than others. For example, the encyclopedia stands out strikingly in what appears an otherwise mundane scene. Often, as in this case, the attraction has to do with an unusualness of image and setting (a lion in the bathroom) or sometimes of the image itself (a winged snake). In both cases the images are "unnatural."

When the dream presents an image that goes against the way things are naturally, let's assume such images to be of high value because they are examples of the *opus contra naturam*. As I understand Jung's idea of symbols, they change the course of nature and upgrade its energy to a higher value. Hence the unnatural, unusual, peculiar image is the one being singled out and the one containing most value.

There is another way of recognizing the value in dream images. Ordinary images may be invested with feeling, e.g., the little brown dog of my childhood or the scarf my mother gave me for Christmas. Here one needs discrimination among feelings – sentiment, kitsch, longing, nostalgia, expectation ... The dream discovers the image of the feeling, exposing the feeling for what it is. So one may read the feeling through the image, as well as the image through the feeling. The dog or the scarf is not only of high value because I feel so strongly about it in my dream, but my dream also tells me where my strong feelings of nostalgia are located. To deal with one's more embarrassing feelings in a dream from a sentimental viewpoint is to miss the embarrassment and therefore the discrimination of the feeling quality.

The case is similar in those situations where one feels the urge to choose between, say, city and country, sky and Earth, family home or own apartment. A dream may show the city as nerve-racking, the country as idyllic, the sky as fearsome, the Earth as nurturing, the family home as complicated and petty, an independent apartment as self-contained and fulfilling. Yet each of these is a fantasy from the point of view of the other. The city looks threatening just because of my idyllic fantasy and vice versa. To choose between one or another of these smaller images is to lose the larger one, which is, after all, a wholeness! To identify with the dream's fantasy, with the terms in which it has presented itself, is to miss the significance of the fantasy.

Structure: Significant structural relationships exist within and among images. Accordingly, images to some extent depend upon each other for their meaning. But it is important here that we separate ourselves from those schools of thought that would see images as *only* structures, deriving their meaning entirely from the slots they fill. In some varieties of structural thinking, form and matter, structure and content, can be separated; in imagistic thinking these pairs are one. The wise old man is both an archetypal structure and a content, and even the number four, the *quaternio*, such an abstract structural idea, is an imagistic content appearing as the four persons of my family, or a four-passenger car, or a city block.

Because images with contents are always structurally positioned within a dream, we cannot speak of them apart from this context. A red bird in one dream and a red bird in another never carry exactly the same content, since neither their structural relation (positioning) within the dream nor the other dream images with which they are structurally related are identical.

And the reverse is also true. Because structures are made up of images with contents, we cannot speak of them apart from these contents. Identical dreams with only a single content different – a black bird rather than a red one – would make for different meanings. In other words, it is not the position alone that makes for a symbol's meaning, but both position and content. The red bird is not the result of structural determinants (laws of force, binary oppositions, grammar, linguistics, or whatever) but is itself one of the determinants shaping the dream. The image is itself an irreducible and complete union of form and content, and for us cannot be considered apart from either. Image is both the content of a structure and the structure of a content.

2. Implication

> Interpretation must guard against making use of any other viewpoints than those manifestly given by the content itself. If someone dreams of a lion, the correct interpretation can only lie in the direction of the lion; in other words, it will be essentially an *amplification* of this image. Anything else would be an inadequate and incorrect interpretation, since the image "lion" is a quite unmistakable and sufficiently positive presentation. [50]
> – C. G. Jung

---

50 CW 17 (above, n. 48), par. 162.

Having set forth the initial aspect of our approach to the dream as image and explored what image *is*, let's move on to its elaboration, what image *implies*. This second means of approach has to do with the entire procedure of drawing implications from the original image. Of course, the further we move from the actual dream text, the more open to question, to individual differences, biases, and particular areas of knowledge (and their accompanying *lacunae*) our interpretation becomes. When we speak of this movement from image to implication (and on to a third category which we shall come to later), we aren't speaking of a sequential progression in the act of interpreting. It isn't that we necessarily look first at image, and then draw implications, and so on, in that order. But these are all aspects of interpretation, whose order is not sequential but ontological. Image is prior not in time, not because we need take it up first when considering a dream, but in the sense of most basic, that to which we return again and again, and that which is the primary ground and spring of our imaginal awareness.

Thus when regarding the dream in its implications, we realize the narrower selectivity within which we are operating. And this seems paradoxical for it feels (because of our greater conceptual development? because of our iconoclastic tradition?) as if the image were the more limited mode. The dream only says this or gives these particular images, while implications seem to extend in many directions. But by moving away from image and into implication we forego the depths of the image – its limitless ambiguities – which can only partly be grasped as implications. So to expand on the dream is also to narrow it – a further reason not to stray too far from the source.

Narrative: We have so far treated the dream in relative stasis, sensing the various events of the dream as its levels or weaves. But now we begin to hear and watch the dream in its narrative or dramatic sense. It was to this aspect of the dream that Jung referred when he spoke of its dramatic structure: setting, development, peripeteia, lysis.[51]

---

51 C. G. Jung, "On the Nature of Dreams," *Structure & Dynamics of the Psyche,* Collected Works, trans. R. F. C. Hull, vol. 8 (Princeton Univ. Press, 1970), par. 561f.

Since most dreams appear in this story form, we might follow Jung here and use narrative rather than image as the primary category. But this brings us into new entanglements, the first of which is the verbal nature of narrative. Even though words contain images, words cannot altogether contain them: words and images are not identical. Since for us images are primary, any form into which the image is cast is a transposition of it, perhaps a step away from it. Of course, putting an image into words can vivify and enhance it; yet, at the same time, this move burdens and informs images with all the problems of language. Language has now become the context, a context that demands its kind of coherence. We nave all had the experience of struggling to write down in coherent form what seems an essentially incoherent dream. But I am beginning to question our idea of coherence. Is it truly the dream that is incoherent or does our verbal approach make it so? Images do not require words to disclose their inherent sense, but as soon as we are involved with language, then what would inhere in the image is transposed into verbal coherence. So we find that some dreams cannot be written down. They resist the transposition, and then we find them "incoherent." We can't put the images together into a story.

So the second difficulty with narrative is that its verbal nature requires a coherence of a special sort: story or a sense of sequence. One thing occurs before another and leads to another. But the sequence of dream fragments is often ambiguous – and from the point of view of the image this must be so, for the image has no before and after. Through our telling, dream fragments whose sequence is ambiguous tend to become one thing rather than another. Our narrating gives an irreversible direction and forms the dream into a definite pattern.

Noting narrative's limitations is not to question the power of the word, the *logos*, in therapy – indeed the way we tell our story is the way we form our therapy – but merely to keep narrative distinct from the more primary imaginal layering and to note their sometimes discrepant phenomenology. When verbal or narrative lapses occur in our dreamtelling, we fill in, we elaborate with what would make sense for narrative meaning, but not necessarily for imagistic meaning. Images are entirely reversible; they have no fixed order or sequence. In some cases these narrative interpolations distort or even betray the image, since they tend to collapse it into the narrative, into the story we tell about it. And if dreams are primarily images – the Greek word for dream, *oneiros*, meant image not story – then putting these images into a narrative is like looking at a painting and making a story of it.

This sense of narration is also reinforced by therapy. As we tell our dreams, so we narrate our life stories. Not only the content of our dreams is influenced by analysis but also the very style of our remembering. Analysis tends to emphasize the narrative rather than the imagistic, even if Jung's emphasis on painting and sculpting has helped restore primacy to the image. But our real concern here is not whether imagistic or narrative report is the more basic. Rather our thought is that since the narrative style of description is inextricably bound with a sense of continuity – what in psychotherapy we call the ego – misuse of continuity because of the ego is also close at hand.

This brings us to the third and most important difficulty of narrative: it tends to become the ego's trip. The hero has a way of finding himself in the midst of any story. He can turn anything into a parable of a way to make it and stay on top. The continuity in a story becomes his ongoing heroic movement. Hence when we read a dream as narrative there is nothing more ego-natural than to take the sequence of movement as a progression culminating in the dreamer's just reward or defeat. The way story encapsulates one into it as protagonist corrupts the dream into a mirror in which the ego sees only its concerns. And since its main concern is progress in terms of whatever value system it has, dream interpretation soon becomes part of the heroic progress. Dreamer and interpreter chop their way through the unconscious – deciding here, refusing there – because the sequence of events has fallen prey to the idea of progressive betterment. Before and after have come also to mean worse and better.

The problem is compounded, since both the dreamer as he appears in the dream and the interpreter's heroic tendencies may appear in more subtle guises than the obvious one of heroic competence. Both may be heroic in function even though they be feeling and submissive. As Hercules dressed in feminine attire at one point, so, too, may heroic consciousness.

But under this submissiveness, ego remains the center of the dream or therapeutic story. The dream is about him, his individuation.

Perhaps what we're really speaking of as heroic-ego consciousness is less one or another mythological figure and more that mode which severs the inherent continuity and intraconnection of the dream image as a whole. This mode continuously makes divisions between good and bad, friends and enemies, positive and negative, in accord with how well these figures and events comply with our notions of progression. Then to interpret as "negative" or "positive" these same characters is to take the narrative at face value, thereby getting caught in the dream ego's idea of movement.

As the failing is a rather obvious one, analytical sophistication has taught us to make one of two contrary moves. We may, for instance, side with the bad guys, taking the viewpoint of the "unconscious" (the forces opposed to the dream ego). Or we may attempt to distance ourselves from the narrative altogether by judging it. We show how the dream situation might have been more adroitly handled, where the ego took a false turn or set up a self-destructive situation. We become coaches, judging performance. But by so judging, we are perhaps even more trapped by the narrative and its ego-emphasis, since this trap is more subtle. Our interpretive remarks about better ways of handling are statements of one heroic and more experienced consciousness (ours) against another (that of the dreamer, who has now been identified with his performance in the dream). We are simply urging him to swap his heroic myth for ours or polish it in terms of ours.

Because the ego bind occasioned by narrative is on some level perhaps inevitable, before going any further we had best pay narrative some of the respect due to it. We cannot hear a story without being caught; we cannot tell a tale without feeling ourselves into some part. Narrative, a most profound mode of archetypal experience, catches us up emotionally and imaginatively. Whether or not we would go so far as to maintain, as some do (e.g. Stephen Crites), that without narrative there would be no experience at all, we can at least agree that tales change experience and enrich daily patterns with archetypal significance. Personal events, moods, jealousies, and even symptoms, when reflected through a story, gain weight and yet distance. Single-sighted life patterns become multidimensional, and the variations brought by the narrative all become part of experience.

But just the reverse is also true when I take, as some part of me always does, the narrative too egoistically, too personally. In this case I become inflated with the archetypal nature of the material, and the material diminishes to fit my ego needs. There is indeed a regressive aspect to *poesis*, a means by which I may merely reinforce my own myopia, may fail to see the fantasy in its far-ranging, autonomous aspect, as not just "mine." When I see it in its archetypal magnitude, judgments fall away. There is no way I can say this character is a good person, this a bad one, this figure made the wrong move, or see how unconscious he was. Characters *are* unconscious. Given the arrangement they all do what they have to do, and given the characters the situation has to be as it is.

Finally, the way we treat narrative is the way we treat our own psyches. To hear the dream story as a moral allegory with a message for right and wrong behavior (progressive, regressive) is to sit in judgment on our souls. When we view the tale as archetypal, however, the characters all become valuable subjective entities, both lesser (only a piece of, not an identity) and greater (with more archetypal resonance) than any of our particular, narrow, and ego-concerned viewpoints.

Amplification: One way we draw upon narrative in analysis is through amplification. Amplifying a dream means an attempt through cultural analogues to make it louder and larger. At first glance it may seem this process mainly calls for a general background of cultural knowledge and some bit of intuition and luck. On closer examination, however, we find the process to be more selective and coherent.

When we ask ourselves what we have done in an amplification, we find first of all *similarities*. A dream figure or theme is in some essential way similar to a mythical figure or theme. The comparison we have made moves us from a personal image to one that is collective and cultural; we have moved from a lesser to a greater, from something fairly known (in the sense of close at hand) to something rather unknown (far-reaching). The key seems to be this quality of *essential* similarity. Whereas a similarity that is merely coincidental would take us very far astray – namely the reams of amplification sometimes used to the detriment of the actual dream – a similarity of essence would of necessity remain in touch with the dream image, which relationship would be expressed in simile ("like" or "as") in order to parallel rather than replace the actual dream image.

Elaboration: Dreams are like knots of condensed implications, which we elaborate by taking key words whose connotations we explicate by treating the words as images. Going westward in a dream becomes going toward freedom, the new, death, sunset, *natura*, clockwise, extraversion... When the dreamer elaborates, or gives associations, there is always the danger of overvaluing them, of letting them be determinate. We tend to forget that his remarks are probably from the conscious point of view; that is, they are ego-syntonic, which does not mean they are invalid, but that they are limited.

In most cases, the dreamer's elaboration tells us more about the dreamer than it does about the dream. We learn from this elaboration the ego's positioning and the constructs through which it views itself. Let's say friend John appears in the text, for whom the dreamer gives the associative attributes of laziness, trickiness, and lack of determination. From this we may assume that the ego's ideal is non-lazy, non-tricky, and determined. But far more importantly, we learn that the dreamer sees *in terms of* these constructs. They say little about the dream, since they are after all conscious elaborations, but tell us a great deal about the ego's relation to the content "friend John."

An oversolicitousness to the associative material may lead us to an additional difficulty in that we may lose to the conscious viewpoint the subtleties of a dream figure. Then we lose the chance to dissolve a conscious fixity, expressed by the association, and instead further rigidify it. The ego and "friend John" become all the more firmly entrenched in the positions they have determined for themselves and each other.

Repetition: This is another characteristic that draws our attention when hearing or reading a dream and from which we draw implications. By repetitions I mean similarities of all and any sort. In the same dream we may find repetitions of adjectives – several things called "great" or "green"; or of verbs – running, rushing, hurrying; or of similarities in shape – a round tire, a round clock face; and so forth. Or the dream may show the recurrence of a theme, for example, lower to higher. Let's say in the dream we find the secretary has no time and one must speak to the boss, a pain in the knee has become now a headache, someone is promoted in school. The collection of these repetitions shows a theme (movement upward) within the dream. This movement cannot be questioned – we can't say it *should* not appear – without betraying the image level of the dream. The most we can do, and it is a great deal, is to point up the repetition and its coordinates: boss, headache, academic promotion. All have to do with an archetypal idea of higher, and each carries the benefits and detriments of the others.

Restatement: The surest way of keeping implications close to the image is by restating the dream and its phrases, giving them a new inflection. By restatement I mean a metaphorical nuance, echoing or reflecting the text beyond its literal statement. This might be done in two ways. First, by replacing the actual word with synonyms and equivalents. (Cf. above under *Elaboration* where the movement westward becomes the movement toward freedom, death, etc.) Second, by simply restating in the same words but emphasizing the metaphorical quality within the words themselves. "I'm driving" in the literal sense becomes "I'm *driving*" or "*I'm* driving," depending on which metaphorical sense we stress. Without restatement we tend to get caught in the dream at its face value and draw easy conclusions from it, never truly entering into the psyche or the dream. When we are completely stumped with a dream, there might be nothing better to do than to replay it, let it sound again, listening until it breaks through into a new key.

3. Supposition

Nowhere do prejudices, misinterpretations, value-judgments, idiosyncrasies, and projections trot themselves out more glibly and unashamedly than in this particular field of research, regardless of whether one is observing oneself or one's neighbour. Nowhere does the observer interfere more drastically with the experiment than in psychology.[52]

– C. G. Jung

---

52 CW 17 (above, n. 48), par. 160.

So far we have spoken of our interpretation in terms of the actual dream text (image) and the implications that can be drawn from it. Now we consider a third category. Supposition, which is most removed from the actual dream text and consequently most open to the personal predilections, opinions, and intuitions of the individual analyst. Under supposition we might place any statement of causality, any "because of this or that" interpretive move; likewise any generalization made on the basis of the dream, any evaluation, prognosis, any use of past or future tense (this will be or this was), as well as any literal advice concerning the analysand's life situation.

Just as in the image all descriptive attributes are interwoven and form a single context, and as our discussion of implication centered in viewing the dream as narrative – so suppositions stem from and involve a single attitude. This attitude feels itself most obliged to have an effect upon the analysand, to give him something, anything at this point, to take home with him. And curiously enough, it seems that the more the other two methods have failed, that is, the more *we* have failed in our imaginative response to the dream – the more insistent our sense that now we must *really* make the connection. Unfortunately our failure with image and implication has probably been due to our own lapses of psyche, our own loss of imaginal reality and sense of soul. And when this occurs, as it seems to so inevitably, our first move toward reclaiming soul is to project it everywhere else and then to *demand* its reality. When the delicate movement of metaphor is lost, we tend to call in stronger, more literal replacements.

Now it seems as though the dream can be made actually relevant only by connecting it with a more simplistic notion of reality, a move made at the cost of the image, whose imaginal reality we can no longer sense. We have lost our touchstone of image as psyche and psyche as image and our premise that nothing can be more relevant or real than the dream image itself. Desperately we attempt to connect the dream to the collective fantasy of a reality we call life, relationships, the workaday world. But curiously enough this move often becomes a move into magic. For by losing the true power of the image, we borrow power instead from a magical connection with the ego-construed world of *materia*.

By magic I here mean: reading the impersonal aspects of the world in terms of my personal intentions and interests (employing dreams for prognosis, diagnosis, foretellings, secret connections ...). One modern form of magical thinking is causal thinking.

Causality: The dream as image makes no causal statements. Events occur in relation to each other but these events are connective, as in painting or sculpture, without being causal. When we make causal statements in our interpretations, as useful as this may be at times, we are no longer talking about the imagination from the imagination, but, rather, from a set of physical suppositions. How we do this makes a difference in our interpretation. In the dream fragment "I'm in a room with Mr. X and suddenly the lights go out" we might say:

(a) X causes the lights to go out. (In rough analytic terms this would be to say that my Shadow X – and all the qualities he carries – causes unconsciousness. So saying, we would then proceed to focus mainly on the agent, Shadow X.)

(b) X is the result of the lights having gone out. (In this case, unconsciousness is a precondition for the appearance of X, and thus we will direct our attention to the unconscious state as agent.)

Let's take another example:

> *My fiancé and I are riding in the mountains in a horse-drawn sleigh. We pull up in front of my mother's house. She sees us and then slams the door so that the horses panic and drag us down a hill at a terrifying pace.*

The most apparent causal statement here is the one given by the dream ego – the mother's door-slamming *causes* the horses to panic. But to take this as the basis for the dream's interpretation is to ignore the total image. My fiancé and I sleighing over the mountain snow could just as well be seen as the cause of my mother's door-slamming or the cause of the horses' panic and downward pull. If we give equal recognition to each aspect of the dream, we realize that all events affect and simultaneously constellate each other. So analytically it is the total situation we must assess, not one or another aspect that, taken causally, would tend to exclude the rest. Perhaps this is the real danger of causal thinking, and why Jung warned of it. When anything is given priority as mover, all others become subsidiary, mere aspects with no more intentionality of their own than billiard balls. Purpose then is imputed only to the initial cause (or causes), and the rest falls into a state without *anima*, without movement or intentionality.

Evaluation: This refers to any negative/positive statement, any value judgment, applied to a dream or to any part of it. On the image level evaluations cannot apply, for the image simply *is*. My mother sticking needles in me is neither positive nor negative; it simply is. In implication, however, with its narrative emphasis, characters take on some quality of – if not good or bad – at least helping or hindering. My mother is hindering me, the protagonist. But this is only because I have the idea of myself as protagonist and therefore require others to position themselves as helping or hindering. Any evaluative idea about my mother's needling behavior – she is a negative character or it is all for my own good – is pure supposition. In our initial dream with the seven interpretive examples, we might likewise suppose that it is good that the dreamer lies down, or it is mere passivity, or that the unknown man is like an intellectualization leading her up and astray, or like a positive *animus* leading her into the unknown regions of her psyche. Which of these we suppose reflects our specific projections upon the dream or our ideas about such things in general.

Generalization: A dream is a specific statement of a particular constellation of characters and settings, so that any attempt to generalize from it is to suppose. Much of what we do in psychology has to do with generalization. We see a specific occurrence or fact and immediately try to give it a general significance, fit it into some larger framework. On the basis of a single dream we tend to say that the dreamer is this or that kind of person or has this or that problem. We make a "working" identity. Generalizations are extremely useful as long as we see that they are merely more or less clever suppositions. But much of what we gain through them we can also accomplish by means of amplification. By amplifying we call up parallels, patterns of significance. In amplification, however, the particular is not lost sight of, is not swallowed by the general, but played alongside, as a second melody in the same key.

Particular dream motifs may easily parallel mythic ones without being subsumed by them.

Specification: Rather connected to generalization is what would seem an opposite. Instead of broadening the dream context, specification refers to its narrowing for specific application. The dream is focused on one or another concern of the dreamer. We say "this dream has to do with the analysis, or your relation to your father, job, marriage…" – the innuendo being what the dreamer should *do* in regard to these matters and that the dream is giving indications. Indeed, we talk about the dream as though it were a theological entity: knowing like an omniscient god, caring like the New Testament God, creating like the Old Testament God, and yet thinking just like you and me. The dream is concerned with all the petty things we are concerned with – where to go, what to do – and then corrects us when we have done the wrong things or made the wrong decisions. Specifying the dream into a message both anthropomorphizes the dream and divinizes it. Whether this be seen as a secularization of the religious instinct, a displacement, or a new wellspring of meaning is entirely up to our theological biases. But whatever stand we take to this theological issue, one thing remains psychologically certain: all specific conclusions we make are in the realm of supposition. The dream doesn't give specific advice; we do, leaning upon the dream for support.

*

When we look back over these suppositions, we find most of what we actually do in therapy falls within this category. We might suppose therefore that dream analysis is highly personal, so much so that interpretations tell more about the interpreter than about the material under scrutiny. And indeed this is so, as we know from the seven different interpretations with which we started. If dream interpretation is so subjective, we might wonder how it works at all.

Just here is the catch – because it does work. What makes it work must be based on something other than the dream image and its implications. Since the relationship between the dream image and our suppositions is so tenuous, we're no longer in a position to claim our interpretations are based on the dream. Their validity must derive from another source, which I suppose we can call therapeutic skill.

Does this mean we have made full circle from our starting point, only to return to the pragmatism with which we began and from which we have tried to escape? If our interpretations are mainly suppositions, and these are successful by virtue of therapeutic skill, then perhaps we must back up our practical ability with a theory of therapy distinct from – that is, no longer disguised as – a theory of dreams. We have made a start in that direction by attempting to recognize and distinguish among our moves in regard to dreams.

When we look back we may also wonder *why* so much of what we do with dreams is supposition. Despite the internal richness of the dream image, or perhaps just because of it, we seem to give least attention to this category. Could it be that we suppose because we cannot imagine? The dream confounds us with the power of its images, and we are mostly at a loss to respond with an equivalent power. Our imaginations are untrained, and we have no adequate epistemology of the imagination with which to meet the dream image on its own level.

Analytical training teaches us primarily how to suppose about dreams and how to work out their implications. We learn by imitating the suppositions of our analysts about our own dreams. What we don't learn is a psychology of the image, comparable to what students of archeology, iconography, aesthetics, or textual criticism would learn about the image in their fields. But we can't even begin to discover what would be a psychology of the image so long as we in psychology are exploiting the image for what we take to be our therapeutic aims. Perhaps the other way round would be more appropriate: discover what the image wants and from that determine our therapy.

But training the imagination and developing an epistemology of it are full of hazards. On the one hand, we have to recognize our historical stuntedness in regard to the imagination, so that when we begin imagining in response to images of dream, literature, or elsewhere, we are not surprised at the impoverishment and the subjectivity of our responses. On the other hand, as if to compensate the iconoclasm of our tradition, there is an undifferentiated glorification of images, which leads neither to precision nor to a psychological connection.

Perhaps the only way through these two limiting alternatives is a *via negativa*, a psychology of the image proceeding from a recognition of unsuitable moves. In this paper I have attempted such an approach. My aim has been to work out a method for interpretive self-awareness, thus to clear some of the confusion from the primary images of the psyche – those that come in dreams. By reflecting upon our interpretive moves vis-a-vis dreams, we may gain some differentiation by realizing when we are not giving due to the imaginal.

V

Defense and Telos in Dreams

Whenever I call something in therapy a "defense," I am at the same time setting up something else as my therapeutic goal. A defense is only such because it defends against this implied goal. For example, if I view my patient as defensively isolated from his surroundings, I am implying interaction with these surroundings as my goal. If I see him as cut off, I am implying connection; if unadapted, adaptation. Defenses make sense only in terms of some therapeutic goal or value.

So to regard defenses in dreams, I must also posit some goal within the dream against which the defense defends. I suggest this goal to be what Jung called the dream's *telos*, the dream's finalistic or purposive aspect, the direction in which it points, that for the sake of which the dream exists.

Internal Telos: Jung distinguished this *telos* or finalistic perspective from Freud's causal, more reductive approach. Freud saw a variety of images appearing as disguises for a central idea to which they could then be reduced, whereas Jung insisted that distinct images are reducible neither to a central idea nor to something known. An image was "more than" anything that could be said about it. For Jung, images opened out, that is, had *telos* or purpose beyond themselves.

Jung's finalistic perspective is valuable not only for individual images, but also for the dream as a whole. That is to say, the dream itself intends something of psychic value; the dream itself has *telos*, purpose, that for the sake of which it exists.

To spot this *telos* within a dream, we must not reduce the dream. One way in which this reduction might occur is by placing the dream's purpose outside the dream. With the *telos* so displaced, we then find ourselves in the curious position of interpreting the dream in terms of a "cause" that doesn't appear in the dream at all. The dream then loses value by being reduced and explained as the result of something outside itself. It is required to fit into larger assumptions and serve a *telos* beyond the dream that has given the dreaming its value.

Let's say, I dream I am having a banquet. If I place the purpose outside the dream I may say something like, "Yes, I dream I am having a banquet and that's because in real life I'm starving." The dream compensates and fulfills the larger assumption of balancing my conscious poverty with inner riches. This interpretation both reduces the dream's precise image to a general abstraction (compensation or balance) and places the reason for the dream's existence, its *telos*, outside the dream. Thus the dream has been robbed of its inherent purpose.

Also, the dream's meaning would then depend upon theoretical attitudes and factual events outside the dream – in this case upon the fact that I am starving and upon the theory of compensation. As these attitudes and events change from day to day and analyst to analyst (according to schools of interpretation), the value of a dream is subject to external vicissitudes. So we get competing interpretations of radically differing positions. Dream interpretation becomes an activity of the "realm of opinion," and the dream becomes arbitrary, subjective, dependent upon the external values to which it is related.

An interpretation of the same dream, *telos* intact, might go rather, "Yes, I dream I am having a banquet because in some part of myself – no matter how miserable my life seems to me – I am nevertheless having a banquet. If this is surprising to me, then I have been missing something."

My intent in this paper is to view the dream as valuable in itself and irreducible to any other factor. I will consider the dream's purpose to be within the dream and will take this purposive movement to be the dream's *telos*. With this value in mind we will eventually have a way of seeing what blocks, stops, or defends against it. But first we need another principle, and for this let us turn to a rule of thumb formulated by the late John Layard.

Layard's Rule: *Nothing in the dream is wrong, except perhaps the dream ego*.[53] Layard's statement gives primary value to the unconscious. All figures and events in the dream, as products of deeper psychic layers, are as they must be. They are genuine psychic expressions. But the dream ego, that by which the dreamer experiences himself, most closely reflects his conscious attitudes. This "I," like consciousness itself, tends to be one-sided and generally blind to deeper considerations, movements, and values. Thus the problems and conflicts in dreams cannot be blamed on one or another psychic figure – which is merely "doing its thing." Rather the dream ego's biases and attitudes must be examined for their role in the conflict.

The Telos Perspective: The Jungian consensus would surely see certain dreams from the perspective I am proposing. For instance, should a dream ego shoot a crowned snake or turn his/her back on a starving child, we would all agree that the dreamer (represented by the dream ego) is unaware of the deeper value of snake or child and is thus behaving in ill accord with the dream's purpose. Our agreement is possible because we have learned from our training the symbolic value of these particular images.

But let us pursue this example into deeper ambiguity – let's say the snake is not crowned, that it appears out of the sewer or in mother's sewing basket, that its color is ugly, murky black, and that it is advancing on the dreamer to swallow him/her.

Here analytical attitudes will begin to divide. Some of us, siding with the dream ego, will view the snake as a threat to be avoided or confronted. Others, backed with amplification concerning the night-sea-journey, will view the same dream as evidence of an important process to be endured.

Possibly everyone at this point, however, would justify his/her view by placing the dream *telos* outside the dream. If the analyst's penchant is for strong, achieving egos and the analysand (a male) is seen as rather

---

53 See also below, 190.

weak in this regard, then the analyst will emphasize the compensatory virtues of snake-battling, standing one's ground, resisting the seduction of being swallowed. The dream would be seen as compensating the life situation of a dreamer who is weak, mother-bound, and passive. Because he is passive, he is in danger of being swallowed. The psyche's intention or *telos* is to awaken the dreamer from that passivity by showing the ugliness of the situation to which he must not succumb. This interpretation of the dream's purpose depends upon our view of the dreamer and upon our general attitude that battling and standing one's ground are better than being swallowed into something unknown.

Although another analyst might view the situation quite differently, nonetheless his/her view would be, just as the first, based upon an external *telos*. Here I am imagining an analyst who does not him/herself fear "being swallowed" and whose sympathies lie much more in exploring rather than battling snakes, mothers, the unconscious. This analyst would be more likely to view the analysand as capable of benefiting from the night-sea-journey (as well as other in-depth psychic experiences). For this analyst the dream would be compensating the dreamer's one-sided, only-conscious, life-involved attitudes by initiating him into something much deeper.

In either case, whatever the analyst's proclivity and however he/she uses the idea of compensation, the *telos* of the dream will have been placed outside the dream, and the dream interpreted from the analyst's suppositions concerning the dreamer, the dreamer's situation, and psychic life in general.

Compensation: Both of the above analysts used an idea of compensation to justify their interpretations. This is possible because compensation can be stretched to cover whatever we wish it to cover.[54] But in either case the explanation by compensation signals that the dream is serving an external purpose. When we focus upon the dream itself – working merely with what is there – reference to compensation becomes unnecessary. It is only when we cannot imagine from and

---

54 CW 8 (above, n. 51), par. 546, where Jung discusses how compensation may oppose, vary upon, or agree with the conscious attitude.

with the dream that we find ourselves speaking of compensation. When an image or dream appears opaque, we tend to leave it and turn to something more general and conceptually familiar. To face the imagistic reality of a swallowing snake, to explore precisely the way this image works in the dream, to feel the anxiety it creates – these are difficult. Far easier to postulate about the dreamer whom the dream must be compensating and about whom we already have ideas.

When we take the dream itself as a reality, as its own context and its own best expression, we find we must dig much more deeply into it. We cannot excuse our imaginative inadequacies by opining about the dreamer's life involvements and personal hang-ups, replacing the dream's reality with what we think the dreamer should be doing about himself, his eros development, his inferior function, his authority problem. Without the idea of compensation ruling us, we may even discover that we have no strong view at all about crowned snakes or ugly snakes and can quite simply take the images of the dream as they come.

Although I seem to be focusing upon analytical bias, that is not my main concern. Of course we all have theoretical positions and make suppositions about the patient. Neither am I primarily concerned with getting to the "objective" truth of the dream in any absolute sense. But I am attempting to stress the dream itself as prior to anything we can suppose about it. By returning to the dream, I hope to clear the way so that we may discern the dream's own *telos*.

The Dream as "Just-So": Because Layard formulated his maxim by emphasizing the dream as "right," we might be led into a too-easy manner of dividing up dream situations. However, *telos* is not a matter of saying "this is right and this wrong," but merely "this is the way it is in this particular psychic situation." The dream is just-so. It's neither right nor wrong. Let's take the following dream fragment as illustration:

> I am wearing a green sweater, but my mother suggests I wear a red one.

That my mother prefers red tells me something about my mother, tells me how she wishes to clothe my upper body in this situation; that I wear green tells me of my ego preference, the attitude I tend to wear. The whole image tells me that my green attitude is worn when her red preference is pronounced. It is not a matter here of choosing one color over another, but of becoming aware of the quality of these two preferences and their interplay as constructs in my psyche.

In an earlier chapter, [55] I suggested "when-then" as a way of viewing this interlinking among images and parts of images. This means that when one thing occurs (my green), another happens as well (my mother's red). Each is a condition for the other. The when-then viewing of images shows them to be psychic patterns, constructs – each part of which constellates the other.

The Layard maxim adds an emphasis or value to this way of viewing by implying that it may be more valuable to explore the mother's red than to reaffirm my own green attitude. As mother's red is furthest from ego attitudes, my habitual and most conscious way of being, mother's red (as more unknown) is what I most need to become aware of. Finalistically, it leads my awareness further into unknowns, hence deeper.

Individuation: What we are calling *telos* might also be regarded as the individuation of the dream. Even in this rather innocuous example, realization of my mother's red leads my psyche beyond the conscious boundaries it has set for itself. My awareness becomes deeper and more differentiated. Viewed in this quite specific manner, individuation becomes an actuality by being imaged in a particular. This is not to speak of individuation as an overall generalization, an abstraction concerned with unions of opposites. Rather, we find ourselves focused upon precise moments as they appear in each dream. This focus brings individuation into the actuality of particular moments.

To regard individuation as a value in every dream gives most credit to the psyche as it actually appears. Moreover, the Layard maxim implies that the tensions and conflicts that appear in dreams (as in life) are necessary, even essential. The psyche is deeply complicated, and its tensions are the means by which it moves. The ego-alien others who give trouble to the dream ego, sometimes torturingly, are at the same time making possible the individuating movement. The tension is the grist by which

---

55 See above, chap. 4, "An Approach to the Dream."

the psyche works, the manner in which it enlarges and differentiates itself. This is an individuation without banners, but it is nevertheless true to the unique personality in all its limitations and particular conflicts. In fact, the shape of these limitations and conflicts is the unique. Individuating is wrestling with the psyche's *telos* – even when this telos runs counter to the ego's natural perspectives and normal behaviors.

Image Values: When we examine images within the dream context, we find we cannot regard any image *per se* as necessarily more important than another or more likely to carry the dream *telos*.

To return to the crowned-snake image, let's pretend the dream went like this:

> There's a crowned snake for which I am the guardian. My job is to
> bring it rats to eat. Suddenly one of the rats attacks and bites me.

Here the crowned snake, though perhaps still a numinous image, is not the carrier of the dream's purpose. Of the two images, rat and snake, the latter is closer to ego consciousness (that which the ego guards); but the rat, less symbolically numinous, traditionally a pest, a "traitor," is here functioning as the dream's *telos*. The crowned snake, as most ego-syntonic, is also most allied with ego defenses; whereas the rat, as ego-alien, carries the dream's *telos*. The ego-defense mechanism involves feeding rats to the crowned snake. Now what might this look like?

Might it be that the dreamer rids himself of his rats – his lowly, scavenger sense of the shadows and the desolated, his instinctual survivors – by giving them over to a majestic, magical, shamanistic aspect of his personality that is more highly valued? As such, this ingesting (rat into snake) is a transformation and a valuable psychic process. But here the emphasis is quite the contrary. The rat instinct rebels, demanding recognition in its own terms – which evidently are not to be crowned-snake terms! No longer may the rat be simply given over to, and swallowed up by, the crowned snake. The defensiveness of this ingestive movement has become apparent through the countermovement of the rat's bite. The rat's attack is upon the dreamer's body. So for the dreamer to be in touch with the rat is also perhaps to be in touch with his body, the means through which the rat has reached him. And vice versa, to be in touch with one's body is to be aware of the realm of the rat – its sense of Shadow and its sense of survival.

Our main point here is that images must be within a context to tell us anything concerning *telos* and defense. Within the larger dream context, images show interconnections and interactions, so that we can then recognize *telos* as that which is more ego-alien and defense as that which is more ego-syntonic. Ego is not threatened by what defends its attitudes and modes of perception, but, rather, by what challenges and disturbs them.

Feeling and Defense: We have seen that a numinous image, like the crowned snake, need not carry the dream *telos*. Nor can we necessarily decide upon this *telos* with our "feeling." Often what feels most right or most important feels so because it is closest to our ego attitudes. Feeling can be as much the ego's statement as thinking or any other mode of apperception.

Feeling is particularly difficult to disentangle, however, because feeling *feels* so personal, so right: feelings are intimately involved with the ego's sense of value and emotional truth – qualities not easily set aside for what sometimes seems an inhuman, unfeeling *telos*. For example, a man dreamt that he had to be given a transfusion of blood from a sick woman. This image feels revolting to our sense of health and our ego expectations concerning treatment and cure. It feels humanly, medically wrong. To take infected blood into one's veins is just too much.

There are indeed many dream images that make us feel appalled or angry or ill. Yet the dream *telos* does sometimes lead into these. To follow the dream we have to admit that the psychic value may lie just where our feelings most rebel. To work with the Layard maxim means that we may not take our first-level, only-natural feelings too literally. In fact, these very feelings – shared by the ego in the dream, and by both the dreamer and the analyst in the session – may be precisely where the defense against the dream *telos* is now hiding.

So the Layard maxim requires a certain delicacy because we all hold our feelings dear and do not want to suspect them. The act of bringing home the value of a repulsive or cruel dream *telos*, against our natural feelings, requires a more subtle feeling attunement and empathy than in those instances that pose no threat. To side against our first and natural feeling requires a differentiation of feeling so as to feel the value of what the psyche values.

Defense and Telos: Freud viewed symptoms as compromise solutions. He meant that symptoms act as safeguards, giving a partial expression to unconscious contents, thereby assuring their continued repression. Imagined physically, this mechanism is like letting some steam from a pot escape so that it doesn't blow its cover entirely. In other words, repression is maintained by relieving some of its pressure in the form of symptoms.

Symptoms are defenses. So, for our purposes, let us hypothesize that *a defense expresses something of the unconscious content from which it would defend itself.* As I put it elsewhere,[56] like not only cures like but like also *defends* against like.

Further, defenses are most effective the more closely they simulate the enemy (from which they would defend themselves). This implies that, if taken far enough, a defense could become indistinguishable from its enemy. By simulating ever more closely, the defense becomes more like that content from which it is, with increasing effectiveness, defending itself.

Let's say I have a cold that simulates my unconscious sense of being "in the cold" and uncared for. My symptom both expresses the unconscious content (being cold and unloved) and defends me from having to recognize that feeling directly. Yet the worse my cold becomes, the more apparent to me that I do in fact need more care. Thus my symptom has led me to the unconscious content from which it had been partly defending me.

Or, to take another example, by placating my mother with simulated love, I defend myself against my deeper love for her; but the more I simulate, with little attentions and gestures, the closer I also come to the content of the love. Or again, let's say I have somatic symptoms that express my feeling of sickness; the more I somaticize in this manner, the closer I come to being actually sick.

---

56 See above, chap. 2, "Neurosis and the Rape of Demeter/Persephone."

By stressing the content of the defense, we have been moving from a Freudian to a more Jungian attitude. We have said that the defense expresses that content from which it would defend itself. Now to take the Jungian leap: each content has *telos*. If a defense expresses unconscious contents (Freud), and if unconscious contents are purposeful (Jung), then, as our title suggested, "defense and *telos* in dreams" have an inherent relation; in fact, the defense is one face of the dream's purpose and necessary to the dream's just-so nature. *The defense is as purposeful as the* telos *itself*

The problem is, of course, that defenses also unfortunately block. However, a defense resists not only because it is a defense and that is what defenses do, but also because it has a hidden value to protect. It, too, expresses the dream's *telos*. So a defense does two apparently contrary things: it carries *telos* and blocks the realization of that *telos*. It both expresses and defends.

Interpenetration of Telos *and* Defense: Our perspective on the relationship of defense and *telos* has by no means provided us with a formula for easy cure. How can we work with a defense that is itself a protector of psychic values? How can we dismantle a defense without at the same time simplifying the purpose of the dream, of which the defense is an integral part? Simply to analyze the defense away would be to destroy the psychic value that it carries.

Also, we have lost the original handles on our inquiry. The two distinctions, *telos* on the one hand and defense on the other, have now become ambiguously mixed. We can no longer claim with the same assurance that *telos* – and only *telos* – is represented in one part of the dream, and defense – and only defense – in another. As much as we would like to say, for instance, that one dream figure was clearly helpful and another defensive, now we must add helpful for what and to whom? Defensive in terms of what? For each figure is going to be in some sense both, and we have relinquished any perspective outside the dream from which to judge. Though we may make initial distinctions between *telos* and defense, these distinctions are only in order to appreciate finally their deeper interpenetration.

Let us put our perspective to practice. The following two images appeared in a man's dream. "I see a hanging, naked, dead woman ... I put on a red dress ..."

À la John Layard, we can start off by saying that the hanging, naked, dead woman is the dream's *telos*. But we must go further; otherwise we would divide *telos* from defense and simply condemn the ego for the wrongness of its red dress. So we go on to say: the first image shows the psychic state (hanging, naked, dead woman) perceived by the dream ego. The second image (I put on a red dress) describes what the dream ego does. When he sees the dead, naked woman, he defends himself by putting on a red dress. His reaction is his resistance against a particularly horrifying image. But still, why this particular defense? The defense involves a "putting on" from the outside, donning an "appearance," which is feminine (a woman's dress), red (an extraverted vibrant color, of visibility, fire, blood, passion). Is the defense like hysteria, implying acting-out and ostentatiousness? Is he in the "habit" of living a manic life in defense against the sense of a dead soul?

Let's assume this to be the nature of the defense, but now for what purpose? Presumably to avoid something that would be more painful or difficult to realize. For this dreamer it is apparently easier to move into the demonstrative show of feminine red clothes than it is to feel the fact of his hanging, dead, unclothed woman. Yet it is a neurotic circle. To reverse the image, it is also *when* he puts on red dresses that his woman is *then* hung-up and naked.

Freud would say that this defense works because it gives partial expression to unconscious forces, therefore compromising the need to change. But Jung would ask what content the symptom (of putting on the red dress) is trying to express. What is its purpose? Its existence cannot be completely negative, "nothing-but" defensive. The dream ego's dressing must also be intending a purpose, pointing toward something.

Most obviously what this defense seems to point toward is woman. And it does so vividly – with red. Yet, also, that from which the dreamer would escape is woman (in the form of a dead, naked, hanging one). So we see that, on a deeper level, *the telos of the defense and the telos of the dream are secretly intertwined.*

Likening: We have viewed the donning of woman's clothes as an attempt to simulate woman. The ego's natural mode of defense has been to liken himself flamboyantly, apotropaically to that which he fears, thus dispelling its deathlike threat. His response has been on the level of appearance (as was Hercules') by wearing woman's clothes. Yet wearing is also bearing, carrying, habituating, giving a style to, fashioning, finding a mode for, taking on with one's body – not just covering as a persona. We need not let the dreamer's "likening" end here as a hysterical put-on. Therapeutically we can deepen the defensive response mimetically through the likeness it has already formed to woman. By wearing woman's clothes, the dreamer has taken on something womanlike. Were he to take on more womanliness in other ways, he would no longer need to live the content defensively and superficially. That is to say, the more the dreamer can recognize the value of the content "woman," the more blood he can give to it, the less hung-up and burdensome it will become, the less it will be a dead concept drying in the air. Then the defense can be relieved of having to be the sole mode of enacting the value of woman.

But in order to relieve the defense carrying the woman-content, we must return to the original image that his ego fears: dead, naked, and hanging. Is her *telos* perhaps her very immobility, hanging gravity, weight, verticality, her unclothed state, her exposure to the air, her suspension (suspended animation), a sense of tragedy of a psychic reality to be lived with? The image sobers, makes grim. When in touch with her, red appearances become pale; put-ons become showy dressing; emotionalized acting-outs show up as pseudo; dramatic expressions appear as mere coverings. In the face of her stark immobility, this image that won't go away, extraverted enactments may slow into ritual and gain the weight of body. "Becoming more feminine," "integrating the *anima,*" may then move from a defensive act of show, the counterpart of a conceptual idea, to a living reality of feeling.

Our model has allowed us to discover a *telos* in the dream ego's defense. Recognition of the purpose in the defense frees it of the values it has had to protect. But for a defense to be so freed, it must first be dismantled with a critical eye to its pathological structure, its too-easy way and secondary gains. Assuredly the defense, invented by Freud, deserves a Freudian treatment. It needs severe reduction and must be brought home as an ego-defense mechanism. But the dream is more than the ego's defense; it is also the psyche's purpose. And this purposefulness may be discovered even in the ego's pathology. For the ego's pathology is inherently in sympathy with the psyche's individuation.

POETICS

VI

Virginities of Image

Since offering the title for this lecture, I have been trying to remember what I meant by it. Whatever my initial intuition, it could not have been an obvious one, for what we mean in imaginal psychology by image is by no means virginal; an image is never pure, never virginal. Even the "idea" of image is unclear. Sometimes we speak of image as though it were a thing, and sometimes we mean by it a way of seeing or hearing.

Image is a complexity of relationships, an inherence of tensions, juxta-positions, and interconnections. An image is neither pure meaning, nor pure relations, nor pure perception. It is not even pure reflection, for one can never say with certainty that this is "the thing" and that a reflection of the thing. Nor can one say that image is *this* literally and *that* metaphori-cally. These dualities – thing *versus* reflection, literal *versus* metaphori-cal – are not images, but, rather, ways of structuring images.

The imaginal is never virginally pure, but always ambiguous, shady, and slightly disreputable, a mixture of shade and light, contour and shadow. With image, modalities intrude. Meanings interpenetrate. Fantasy and perception break into each other. Idea and fact transgress each other's borders. The virginal resists these intrusions, these inter-penetrations, these impurities. In this sense we can say that the virgin is that which resists the imagistic. And this is my first main theme: *to resist the image is to be virginal in psyche, and to be a psychic virgin is to be closed to the image.*

Resistance is necessary for the virginal integrity of the body of the image. Image is a body – a psychic body that holds tension and supports being. Though we foolishly interpret, simplistically allegorize, reduce meanings to symbols and signs, the image remains – never changing, never yielding. Like the inscrutable, virginal sphinx,[57] the image puzzles us with questions, but yields no answers.

Resistance has different forms, and the virginal can resist in many ways. Resistance may take the form of the virgin Hippolytus, for whom virginity means *exclusivity* – the exclusive worship of one divinity. Hippolytus is dedicated solely to the chaste, free spirit of Artemis. He rejects the Aphroditic that would entangle him in the complications of sensuality and erotic involvement. Hippolytus is interested in distant beauty – not sensuality, an intercourse that would allow the image to move in and through him. He enjoys hunting the image (tracking it down), but not its embrace. Hippolytus does not realize that he is in image, but sees image as something remote to be pursued. His far-ranging spirit remains unfettered and chaste, pure and keen-sighted in the distant, free realm of the woods. Artemisian spirit is indeed part of image: free as its spontaneity, its hidden life, its appeal to our curiosity. But the exclusive worship of this freedom, distance, and curiosity is doomed to fail in the myth of Hippolytus – doomed to fail tragically.

Now what can we make of this pattern in terms of image? We are familiar with images that present this free, soaring, Artemisian sense: images seemingly unconnected with civilization and society, the close-at-hand, the near – those small, involving details, the entanglements of daily life we experience with family, spouse, children, acquaintances. For a votary of Artemis, image embodies none of these entanglements. Hippolytus is appreciative and reverent, but, at the same time, untouched, not embodied by the body of image.

When one is fascinated by this ephemeral, Artemisian aspect of image, sight becomes far-sighted; implications become far-reaching like

---

57 The sphinx was called *parthenos*, "virgin." See Roscher, *Ausführliches Lexikon* (above, n. 35), s.v.

Artemis's arrows. Feelings soar impersonally beyond the here-and-now, above the tangles of the immediate, the mess of the petty, personal details of everyday life. Here is an account by an American woman in Europe of a dream that captures something of this feeling:

> I was standing in line at the Zentralbibliothek in Zurich to get a book. I realized that the language everyone was speaking was a dialect I didn't understand. I panicked, wondering how I was going to ask for the books I needed. A tall woman came up to me and, putting her arm around me, took me past the line and up to the window to get the books. We then walked together through the streets. It was night. I felt elated that I'd been able to finish my research. Tremendous freedom. We walked what seemed like all night, as though through an amusement park. Lights flashed, things twirled and flickered in the distance like rides (roller coasters, Ferris wheels, etc.). Then she took me into a harshly-lit cafeteria. The place was ugly and the people shabby. Suddenly she put her arm around me and put her hand into my pants. I was horrified and pushed her away violently.

The tone of the first part of this dream is Artemisian. A tall woman figure guides the dreamer to the books she desires. The dreamer feels inspired and free; her spirit soars. Amusement lights flash and flicker – in the distance, notice, not the nearness. Then the whole scene turns, and in the not-so-clean well-lit place (where food is served in harsh light), the woman who hitherto had been a spirited Artemisian guide now turns, in a most un-Artemisian way, grossly physical. The virginally pure aspect of the image seems to have turned upon itself and shifted downward, focusing inappropriately below the belt. The image has plunged from its highflying, inspirational virginity, shocking the dreamer into an awareness that her body is also part of the situation. The body, the sexual, forms part of the image – finding the book is also being found in the body and being harshly violated.

Interpreting this dream, one can easily be caught by its virginal spirit and thus side exclusively (purely, virginally) with one aspect of the dream – depending on the penchant of the analyst, with either the "up-ward," nonphysical or the "downward," physical, grosser aspect. But an image includes all of its aspects, as the dream shows. The woman fig-ure who inspires the spirit at the same time lowers the dreamer into her lower nature through the impurity of sexuality.

The virginal may appear in another pattern of image work. The vir-gin Narcissus reflects endlessly, purely upon himself. As the clear pool of this reflection ripples in depth. Narcissus raptures ever deeper. The movement is profound. Narcissistic reflection is deeply self-revealing and self-contained, alchemically enclosed within the narrow limits of the pond. But despite this depth of vertical reflection, or perhaps because of it, the horizontal world of Echo is ignored. In the tale. Echo pines away, longing for the narcissistic reflection that excludes her. Let us say that Echo is the echoing of what is "out-there" – objects, the daily, others, the lateral. Narcissus ignores these reverberations from surfaces, things around. Attempting to find insight and meaning within oneself, one be-comes deaf to surroundings.

Image work seems to invite this narcissistic virginity. Because re-flection and depth are so vitally important, image tends to draw one into "vertical" rather than "horizontal" reflection. But the Lopez max-im, "stick to the image," does not necessitate a mesmerized downward stare. Depth can also mean a depth within, a penetration of the imme-diate across and through surfaces.

Narcissus, unlike other virgins, does not flee from the physical; rath-er, he flees into it. It is the less physical realm of sounds and echoes that he fears. As sound, Echo cannot be touched; it cannot be concretized. The essence of Echo is precisely in the reverberations, the hiatus, the space between. Whereas the image can remain virginal if it is held – nar-cissistically – too close, Echo requires distance, breadth.

Dreams in which one is rejected, betrayed, failed, or made jealous create the distance needed for echo to sound. In these dreams, emp-tiness is created, room established, attachments dissolved, sensual-ity irrelevant. The movement is one of echoing out of oneself, beyond physical attachments, and attachments to the physical, into a broader, more substantial, wider-ranging world.

The virgin Cassandra offers us another pattern of the virginal. Whereas Hippolytus denies Aphroditic consciousness (and Narcissus, Echo's), Cassandra resists the Apollonic. Apollo, in his passion for Cassandra, bestows on her the gift of prophecy. But when Cassandra refuses him, preferring to remain virginally untouched, Apollo swears that none shall believe her prophecies. Cassandra's virginity denies Apollonic consciousness, denies the formality and clarity of image work, denies that ideas can be abstracted from images, connections made, thoughts formed, things structured.

Sometimes dreams speak quite directly about the necessity of form. For example, an analysand having difficulty writing a paper dreamt that she was sitting in her office writing when suddenly she heard crying. Huddled in the corner was a black woman who, sobbing, held up a string of African beads.

It would seem that the sobbing woman made a direct appeal concerning form. The manner in which the analysand was writing evidently hurt the black woman, who offered another mode more loosely connected, like beads on a string. Structure need not be logically deductive, but might be, as in this case, circular and still be formally exact.

In general one might say that images contain particular forms, that there is a formal element within the image. But Cassandra virginity denies this formality so that attempts to bring out the structure of a thought or image seem a violation: a dream too precious to be written down, feelings too deep to be spoken, intuitions too subtle to be articulated. When one is in this virginal mood, Apollonic clarity and exactitude feel threatening, "just academic" or "only a head trip." Cassandra needs to be misunderstood. Her perceptions and intuitions do not lack insight. In truth, they are quite acute, but they lack effect, the power of persuasion, or *peitho*.

Peitho is important. In Aeschylus's *Agamemnon* it is not that Cassandra's words go unheard – the chorus hears what she is saying – but her words have no *effect*; her prophecies do not touch the principal characters or influence the course of action. This inability to influence, to formulate effectively, is Cassandra's purity.

Of course, we all have something of this virginity – particularly when we turn prophetic. Thoughts that have no effect in the here-and-now get projected into the future. When "what-is" lacks persuasiveness, it becomes "what *will be*" in the guise of literal foretelling or warning.

In analysis we tend to make these prophetic or prognostic declamations when we cannot articulate the material. When an image in a dream fails to convey a sense of psychic reality, or when our feelings for the dream lack *peitho*, we tend to project this lack as a power into the future. Cassandra's virginity, by running from formal articulation, loses touch with the persuasive power of the image.

We have mentioned now three mythic patterns of virginity: Hippolytus. Narcissus, and Cassandra. All have in common an absence of body in relation to image – whether that absence is of the physical body (as in the case of Hippolytus), or the body as world (Narcissus), or the body of form and persuasion (Cassandra). In each instance, the body aspect of image remains untouched, so that the virginity of psyche is untouched by the image.

In addition to these mythic styles of virginity, let us turn to some aesthetic styles; for these I call upon poetry, an art that has long dealt with the subtleties and problems of image. But poetry, too, has a virginal aspect. As Robert Penn Warren observes in his essay "Pure and Impure Poetry,"[58] if a poem were entirely pure (in our terms, virginal), it would no longer be a poem; a good or complete poem requires impurity.

Warren's idea holds not only for the poetics of poetry, but also for the poetics of psyche; that is, for the poetics of dreams. Of course, there are differences between poems and dreams, but let us look at their poetic similarities. Consider Shelley's "The Cloud":

> I bring fresh showers for the thirsting flowers,
>   From the seas and the streams;
> I bear light shade for the leaves when laid
>   In their noonday dreams.
> From my wings are shaken the dews that waken

---

58 R. P. Warren, "Pure and Impure Poetry," in *Critical Theory Since Plato*, ed. H. Adams (New York: Harcourt Brace Jovanovich, 1971), 981–92.

The sweet buds every one,
When rocked to rest on their mother's breast,
As she dances about the sun. [59]

Now in terms of image these are fairly insubstantial lines. They lack irony or, in psychological terms, have little self-awareness or reflective consciousness. Poetically, they acquire some tension through form and rhyme scheme. But this tension is not particularly fertile. The "I" who is the cloud simply carries on powerfully and descriptively, with little trouble or complication.

Now let me read you part of a dream that seems comparable. The dreamer is a woman in her thirties.

I came to a building site and had difficulty going on because there
was a big bulldozer with iron, bladelike teeth. The driver did not see
me for it kept coming very near. Then I began dancing. As I danced
I felt great power and magic and the machine was driven away.

The dream tells of a dancing ego personality, the "I" in the dream, so powerful in her charm that she dances away the bulldozer – a building machine that would clear the ground and prepare the virginal earth for construction. The power of the dreamer's magic dance keeps all this potential work of the bulldozer at bay. The dream reveals an effective defense.

As you might imagine, the dreamer was a *femme fatale* – magical, mediumistic, and powerful – who had literally seduced her way through life's difficulties. Her dance knew no limits. Whatever threatened her she slept with. But this magical dance had also kept her virginal, effectively blocking the process of construction, any encroachment of civilization or culture.

Both dream and poem have a kind of tension – the poem in its form and the dream in its content: dancer threatened by bulldozer. But both dream and poem remain virginal images because they lack a crucial

---

59 *Shelley: Selected Poetry* (London: Penguin Books, 1956), 179.

kind of tension, what Susanne Langer would call "fecundity."[60] A fecund tension breaks through the surface of what is happening and creates a surprising, difficult, or unaccustomed moment. The virginity of an image is not deflowered by just any kind of tension, but only by a fecund tension, a tension that does something, that turns the Earth or surprises the cloud, breaks through the accustomed. If an image is not to remain virginal, it needs this fecund tension.

Let us turn now to another mode of the aesthetic virginal: the virginal as self-same or self-enclosed. As an example of this virginity, note a poem by Walter Savage Landor entitled "Dying Speech of an Old Philosopher":

> I strove with none, for none was worth my strife:
> Nature I loved, and, next to Nature, Art:
> I warm'd both hands before the fire of Life;
> It sinks; and I am ready to depart.[61]

The poem is self-enclosed, so that even as death approaches we find nothing abrupt or jagged, nothing cacophonous. The poem remains at one with its feeling, unruffled, and relatively uninteresting. As a virginal image, the poem is an idealized mood.

Compare this with another of Landor's poems on the theme of death. This poem, too, begins virginally:

> Mild is the parting year, and sweet
> The odour of the falling spray;
> Life passes on more rudely fleet.
> And balmless is its closing day.

This poem, in contrast to the first, begins to show complexity in its juxtaposition of "rudely fleet" and "balmless." It goes on to describe the close of life:

60 Susanne Langer speaks of the "principle of fecundity," by which she means that an idea must be not only true but interesting. See her *Feeling and Form* (New York: Scribner's, 1953).

61 *Representative Poetry Online* (University of Toronto Libraries), http://rpo.library.utoronto.ca/poem/1216.html (accessed August 26, 2008).

I wait its close, I court its gloom,
   But mourn that never must there fall
   Or on my breast or on my tomb
   The tear that would have soothed it all. [62]

The poem's initial virginity is effectively broken by the last stanza. Progressively, the simple perception of the first lines is interpenetrated by more complex emotions. In the second stanza, the "I" waits its close, courts its gloom, and mourns. Waiting, courting, and mourning are three quite distinct emotions, any of which alone might be merely virginal. In succession, however, the movement becomes increasingly complex as each feeling breaks apart or opens the previous.

This nonvirginal complexity is certainly a psychological achievement. It is not ambivalence; the poem is quite firm in its direction. Nor is it complexity for the sake of complexity. At this point, it would be easy to say that complexity in itself is the nonvirginal and therefore our aim. But there are all sorts of complexity, including the simply associative or decorative. The virgin bedecked with jewels and robes, halos, embroidery, and glitter may *appear* "complex," but she is not necessarily transformative. An ornate baroque image is not necessarily more interesting than, say, a simple, classic one, on the sole ground that the one image is complex and the other is not. Similarly, psychological associations, esoteric amplifications, and symbols do not by themselves transform virginity, but may merely adorn and cover it further. We must not confuse the fecundity of an image with complications that have been added to it.

Indeed, the nonvirginal may be quite simple – as imagistic poetry or haiku is simple. The simple may also be the essential. William Carlos Williams's "red wheel / barrow / glazed with rain" [63] is terse, but this terseness crystallizes. The refined condensations that we find in imagistic poetry and in the most beautiful calligraphy are achievements of

---

62 Ibid., http://rpo.library.utoronto.ca/poem/1219.html (accessed August 26, 2008)

63 *The Collected Poems of William Carlos Williams, Vol. 1: 1909–1939*, ed. A. Walton Litz and C. MacGowan (New York: New Directions, 1986), 224.

essence, highly refined moments. The simple is not always the simplistic or subjective, as critics of imagism maintain. [64]

As virginal, the image holds something "more-than" the simple or innocent; it contains something divine. Not only the Virgin Mary, but also most pagan goddesses carry the epithet *parthenos*, or "virgin." [65] Athena, Artemis, Persephone, Hestia – but also Hera and Aphrodite – are called *parthenos*. Hera the wife and Aphrodite the lover have virginal qualities. As these divine figures psychologically encompass more than mere biology, so, too, does virginity refer to a psychic state.

For the Greeks, any child born of an unmarried mother was considered virginal. [66] The epithet *parthenos* applied to the children of concubines or prostitutes – indeed any child whose "father" was not the man in the living room. In other words, the father of the virgin is the absent, the unknown, or the spirit "father." [67]

The father of a virginal image cannot be known. Our petty inquiries into the "history" of a poem, our researches into influences or the author's biography, our attempts to determine cultural causes and personal traumas, to detail the "affective needs" that a poem satisfies – all miss the point. [68] And psychology, which should perhaps know most about this virginal state of the psyche, is often most ignorant, insensitive, positivistic, and causalistic about it.

When working with dreams, we sometimes disparage a simple scene or statement by calling it a dream fragment. These "fragments" often embarrass the dreamer, as though there *should* be more, as though our

---

64 As an example of criticism that confuses the simple with the simplistic, see P. Wheelwright, *Metaphor and Reality* (Bloomington/London: Indiana Univ. Press, 1968), 159ff.

65 See above, n.56. See also J. M. Robertson, *Christianity and Mythology*, 2nd ed. (London: Watts & Co., 1910), 293. Robertson's list includes Aphrodite, Hera, Demeter, Cybele, Leto, and Isis.

66 H. G. Liddell and R. Scott, *A Greek-English Lexicon* (Oxford Univ. Press, 1996), s.v. "Parthenios."

67 See J. Layard, *The Virgin Archetype* (New York and Zurich: Spring Publications, 1977), 288ff., on the connection between virgin and spirit.

68 In this regard, see the essays by Hippolyte Taine, Sigmund Freud, and I. A. Richards in *Critical Theory Since Plato* (above, n.57).

psyches should be interestingly complex and engaged with fascinating symbols. These analytical judgments are comparable, in literary terms, to the judgment of one genre in terms of another – to the view of an imagistic poem, say, from the perspective of a rambling Dostoevsky narrative; or, in our terms, to the view of the dream, a product of Hades, from the perspective of a tumbling, ever-fluid life.

Imagism in dreams may show as depressive. In such moments, the psyche appears tightened, coagulated, stuck without movement. Psychic imagism can thus be the poetic cure for too much life by returning us to what is tight, essential, and bonelike. Dreams of death, dying, deserts, dreams of consuming or being consumed, blocked, imprisoned, constrained, stopped, or parched express the importance of this psychic process. Here, again, the simple, imagistically sparse is by no means the virginal.

In fact, the virginal may appear as quite the contrary. Virginity can be fluid, flirtatious, loquacious, bubbly, and pointless; it can be fiery, quick, and fantastic. There are dreams in which so much seems to happen and yet little does, despite the apparently transformative imagery, as in the following: *A hawk with a mickey-mouse mask dove at me... it turned into flames that then turned blue and green and then with clutching, handlike movements climbed up a telephone pole.*

Fantastical dreams seem to be working to turn natural perception into more complicated perception by means of the unnatural or surrealistic. It is as though perception is working on itself in an attempt to make a psychological difference. But insofar as this difference is only fantastical, the psyche is still virginal, as though fascinated with its own frivolousness.

The following lines show the fantastical combined with subjectivism:

> I am the cause, I am a stockpile of chemical
> toys, my body
> is a deadly gadget,
> I reach out in love, my hands are guns,
> my good intentions are completely lethal. [69]

---

69 "It is dangerous to read newspapers," in *Margaret Atwood: Selected Poems,*

Here the lethal has been exaggerated to the fantastic and then infused with subjectivity. The poet has identified with the lethal as though the world of warfare were one with subjective feeling. T. S. Eliot's warning concerning the personal is important here: "Poetry is not a turning loose of emotion, but an escape from emotion; it is not the expression of personality, but an escape from personality."[70] The poem must be depersonalized or at least more distant and complex than personal, subjective feelings.

The virginal, as we have seen, is a fantastic, personal, or simplistic quality of mind. Aesthetically as well as psychologically, the virginal is an innocence, a naivete to be penetrated psychologically and worked artistically. But we have also implied that the virginal is part of the image. I would now add that *the virgin is not only part of, but even crucial to the image.* We have imagined the virginal as resistance, an aspect of the psyche that wishes not to yield. But while resisting intrusion, the virgin also gives it form; that is, the purity in the image gives the image form. The way in which a poem is pure – fantastically, simplistically, or subjectively – requires particular artistic moves, particular kinds of impurity for the poem to cohere.

For an application of these moves to dreams, we can recall the example of the dancer and the bulldozer. At the narrative level, we might say that the dancer drove the bulldozer away. Imagistically (or from the point of view of image), however, we can also say that the dancer is the occasion of the machine's coming; both occur together. The seductress and the bulldozer each form part of the building site. The dancer is also a condition/or construction.

A fecund tension is required. The psyche needs tension to create the intensity with which to work. And the purity of the virgin's resistance is crucial to this intensity.

The virgin is "uptight" because the virgin indeed has something to protect: a dedication to the impersonal and its values. As the virginal

1965–1975 (Boston: Mariner Books/Houghton Mifflin Company, 1976), 59.

70 T. S. Eliot, "Tradition and the Individual Talent," in *Critical Theory Since Plato* (above, n.57),

aspect in a poem protects the poem, so in a dream it protects the dream. The icon of the virgin on the wall, the image of the virgin as symbol, is testament to the eternal virginity of image, its pure and inviolate nature. The virgin depicts not only the image of virginity, but the virginity of image intact unto itself.

The virgin of unknown father, as virgin mother, is self-generative. This parthenogenesis is the generativity of the imagination. Yet – and I would not want to end without some final conundrum – the virgin is virginal only insofar as there is something that is also nonvirginal: the *beata culpa.* Imagistically, purity and impurity go hand-in-hand. It is the impurity of an image or a poem that protects its purity. T. S. Eliot's *Waste Land* ends with *shantih, shantih, shantih –* a feeling of pure but hard-earned peace. These final lines of *shantih* ring with such beauty, integrity – and virginity – because of the extraordinary impurity of the poem that has preceded: the "heap of broken images," the "wrinkled dugs," the rat "dragging its slimy belly on the bank" – a teeming richness of complex, sophisticated impurity that readies us for a peace of integrity. This is not the simplistic peace of a virgin – naive, innocent, unspoilt – but the peace of an imaginal achievement. Alchemically, this is not the virgin as *prima materia* (the milky unconscious), but the virgin as a recovery of something worked.

William Butler Yeats, at the age of seventy-two, wrote in one of his last poems:

> Those masterful images because complete
> Grew in pure mind but out of what began?
> A mound of refuse or the sweepings of a street,
> Old kettles, old bottles, and a broken can,
> Old iron, old bones, old rags, that raving slut
> Who keeps the till. Now that my ladder's gone
> I must lie down where all the ladders start,
> In the foul rag and bone shop of the heart.[71]

---

71 From "The Circus Animals' Desertion," in *The Collected Works of W. B. Yeats,* vol. 1: The Poems, ed. R. J. Finneran (New York: Scribners,1997), 356.

The pure of which Yeats speaks would seem the virginal achievement of image. The mound of refuse, the raving slut, the foul rag-and-bone shop of the heart are the impurities that give integrity to the virginity of the image.

VII

Echo's Passion

Little has been written on the figure of Echo, and those who have commented tend to regard her negatively. These comments cluster in themes: (1) Echo has a self-defeating passion. She is in love with an unattainable object (Narcissus). This is an impossible love, since Narcissus continually rejects her. Echo in this view is a kind of masochist. (2) Echo lacks an identity; since she can only echo what others have said, she has no identity of her own. She (3) is only responsive, (4) merely mimics, (5) never originates.

What about this identity that Echo lacks? The idea of "identity" is very trendy in current psychology. "Just be yourself," we say, as though one could step into something called "self," as though whatever else one is doing is not one's self, but something other. Self-identity implies an entity distinct from surroundings and other persons. It implies an essential sameness, oneness, and internal unity of personality.

The commentators are right. Echo is not selfsame or one; nor is she separate from her surroundings. (She needs surroundings in order to speak.) Psychiatrically, Echo has indeed a very poor sense of identity. Further, her boundaries are so loose that she has been, at one time or another, involved with everything – literally everything. She calls this everything "Pan." Echo has been a lover of Pan, whose name means "all," everything. But to be imagistically more precise, Pan is a determinate kind of everything. (Even everything, the all, comes as a particular image.) Pan is a hairy, goatlike, lustful everything. We could say that

Pan is that desirous animal force that claims itself to be everything, presents himself as though he were everything. So when the lust of Pan is constellated, it feels like everything – as if that's all that's important. (This leads easily, by the way, to panic. When something is all-important, it is on the edge of panic as well.)

Pan desires Echo. One could say that all that's desirous, this everything that desires, desires an echoing. Within desire, within Pan's passion, is a passion for Echo.

But Echo doesn't feel the same way. In the tale, she flees Pan. Echo rejects the demand that everything be echoed. Though I said a moment ago that Echo is involved with everything, part of this involvement is also a resistance, a flight away from responding to all and everything.

Just what does Echo desire? If "everything" doesn't attract her, what does? She desires a single thing, a single self-enclosed young man – Narcissus. We could say that Echo desires the singular, the narcissistically self-contained, that which is self-enclosed by its own image. She can echo only that which is imaged, not everything all over the place, but this, the particular within its self-containment.

In psychological work one feels how everything wants Echo, and yet Echo herself doesn't seem to want that; how Echo wants particulars, not generalities; and how Echo may want to echo this-but-not-that. You can't be psychological everywhere! (To do so would be a kind of rape of Echo.)

It's as though one has to be unpsychological most of the time in order to be psychological some of the time – as though one has to be naive, direct, instinctual on a Pan level in order to serve Echo in those particular places (in those particular moments) where she truly echoes.

Echo is a rarity – she's not one with Pan's natural world. She doesn't unite with it. She's in this way unnatural, contra-natural.

Certainly there's much more echo in "unnatural" occurrences – in symptoms, say, or perversions – than in things that work normally. (Analysts love unnatural things because that's when we can begin to hear. When things get weird, unnatural, disunited, you can begin to hear them.) So Echo doesn't make it with Pan because that would be too natural. She has other things to do – such as deceive Juno. Let me quote the lines from Ovid (in Louise Vinge's translation) about this deception:

> ... often when Juno might have surprised the nymphs in company with
> her lord upon the mountain-sides, Echo would cunningly hold the god-
> dess in long talk until the nymphs were fled. When Saturnia realized
> this, she said, "That tongue of thine, by which I have been tricked, shall
> have its power curtailed and enjoy only the briefest use of speech."[72]

So Hera curses Echo. Now who is Hera?

Hera is a queen, a ruler, a ruling mode of consciousness, and like
her husband, Zeus, concerned with the wider realm of things. Her penchant is for fact, form, and order, and so she is a great literalizer. For
Hera what occurs must really occur as *actual* within the social order of
things (the debutante ball, the bar mitzvah, the engagement party). Hera
serves the establishment, serves to make things established. Beauty in
the realm of Hera is what shows in the social world, what is actually
manifestly "out there." Hera's beauty in the world is thus quite different
from Echo's more insubstantial, delicate, indirect sense of beauty.

Echo's aesthetic occurs in the empty spaces, the caverns. This emp-
tiness – the emptiness in an event, the lack in a manifestation – gives
shape to Echo. This echoing of the empty is of course threatening to
Hera because it cheats her more definite, established reality by showing the hollowness within it. Take Hera's ideas of marriage: for Hera,
marriage is one-to-one, all wrapped up, solid, no gaps. Echo searches
out the holes, the hollows, within which there are indeed many echoing
possibilities.

While Echo talks with Hera in the Ovid passage, a free-love fertility
occurs in the background (Zeus making love with the nymphs). Echo's
words cover things, hide things from Hera awareness, making possible
activities beneath the expected, manifested order. So words, Echo's
words, make possible, at the same time, a certain covert fertility.

This brings us to words. For Hera, words are facts. "Well, did you,
or didn't you?" And if a word's not a fact, then it's all just talk. Hera is
a kind of nominalist concerning language. Words are empty or refer

---

72 *Metamorphoses* 3.360–65.

to facts. For Echo (to echo it again), words are neither just words nor just facts, but, rather, fertile, seductive, procreative. Within words, behind words, Zeus is always making love with the nymphs. As one talks, fertile, procreative, echoing things are also occurring in the background.

We noted earlier that Echo is not an originator (we said she has no identity). Nevertheless, as we see here, she plays an important role in making origination possible. When Echo talks, Hera is distracted. And when Hera is distracted, Zeus originates, conceiving new forms and possibilities. Indeed, he gives rise to most of the gods and goddesses in this contra-Hera manner. (Most of the divinities are Zeus's bastards.) Though Zeus and Hera are the veritable archetype of marriage, most of the fruits of that union are occurring in the hollows beneath (or apart from) their married intention, not apart from their marriage necessarily, but apart from its conscious intention.

And now we have to give Hera more credit. She, too, is a divinity; even her inability to understand what's happening is important. Perhaps it's important that the established not understand the unformed and the unestablished. In this way, a tension is maintained – a tension between form, continuity, the manifest, the past, the tradition on the one hand, and the miscreant, the upstart, the bastardly, the new on the other. This tension is what gives the new its sense as something odd (and original) and also requires of the new that it too come formally to terms, at some time or another, in one manner or another.

Of course, one way of coming to terms with Hera is negatively, by being cursed. Without form, without the curse of form, Echo is merely chatter. (Echo merely chats with Hera.) This stage of Echo is like the telling of a long-winded story – a series of unreflected, un-shaped details in which nothing stands out, nothing recedes. There are no levels of voice, so that all is of the same import.

As we all know, this kind of talk numbs one's sense of form, and in the tale Hera forgets what she's about, forgets to attend. This forgetfulness is (in a perverse sort of way) erotic, seductive – it allows Zeus and the nymphs to make merry in the tangled hollows beneath the story. So boring stories are really quite important. It's Hera's way of relaxing her awareness. Through gossip, bridge-party trivialities, and such talk, Hera awareness is relaxed so that something can occur beneath it.

The artist Andy Warhol was adept at capturing in his films this talkative, nonsensical, erotic level of awareness. Warhol's characters (who are all in rebellion against Hera) talk continuously and seduce at the same time. Quite literally, as they make love, they also talk nonstop.

So we have Echo in her preformed, verbose stage. When Hera comes to, however, and realizes what is happening, she curses Echo not only with form, but with a double dose of formal adherence. Echo must now form in the strictest possible manner, through actual repetition – or repetition of the actual.

A word then about repetition. Repetition would seem a fairly important business. Psychiatry speaks of the repetition compulsion, of echolalia, of the tendency of neurosis to repeat the same patterns again and again. Jung sees verbal repetition (in his association experiment) as a complex indicator. And, of course, even in everyday behavior we all repeat. We tell the same stories over and over. We all have certain phrases that we can't seem to stop saying. And these repetitions are fairly embarrassing because they show our lack of originality. No one wants to be an Echo. But how is it that we don't take better care not to repeat? Have we some deep investment in our repetitions – some love for them? Is there a beauty there? To "learn by heart" – repetition goes to the heart, comes from the heart – it is deep-seated.

Alchemically one might speak of this loyalty to the repetition as the *iteratio*, the necessity of doing the same operation again. One swallow doesn't make a summer, say the alchemists; one poem doesn't make a poet, say the poets. We need to do it again; we're driven to repeat it.

This repetition may be Echo's attempt at continuity, her kind of continuity. (What's continuous? What recurs.) The duration of Hera that Echo lacks returns as Echo's repetitions, so that Echo is no longer merely flitting, flirting, but reworking through repeating the same words.

Repetition is also an attempt to make something take. If we say something often enough, it becomes more essential and characteristic; we begin to believe what we repeat. In the Underworld, repetition also expresses essence – the essence of a character (Tantalus, Ixion, Sisyphus...).

If there seems to be beauty in repetition, some of it is, I think, tied up with Narcissus. We repeat what we find self-reflectively beautiful. Narcissus longs deeply (or longs to deepen) the beauty of this self-reflection. His longing is downward into the pool, toward his reflection in depth.

What we love, what we long for, tells us something of ourselves. Even our mannerisms, our cute phrases, our verbal and behavioral oddities are telling. "You know what I mean?" I repeat as though crucial to know, to be known to myself. Repetitions are longings for Narcissus, for self-reflection.

I have a friend who uses a peculiar phrase. He speaks of "teasing apart" an idea in order to make a distinction. "Teasing apart," he says again and again, as though this flirtatious, sensual metaphor were in some way crucial to what he longs for, to his rationality becoming also teasing and delicate – flirtatious like a lover. I think this self-reflective teasing is the Narcissus within his work, attracting him to it, attempting to bring to it a deeper level of beauty and sensuality.

My general point here is that repetitions are strangely durable, and though they appear superficial, they nonetheless point toward some deeper need. Echo longs for this beauty of self-reflected depth.

Words contain an interplay between Echo and Narcissus. Words circle within themselves aesthetically and self-reflectively. Through alliteration, rhyme, vowel and consonant patterns, and beat, words are aesthetically autogenerative. If they were not – if words were instead healthy and related and object-oriented, communicating directly and unambiguously from me to you – they would be merely Hera words or signs ("televisionese," *Reader's Digest*, academic talk). They would not be words of an aesthetic self-longing.

Further, there is a certain erotic value in de-emphasizing the literal nature of words. Echo is a nymph in love, and when one is in love, words at face value mean little. "I love you," "I don't love you," or "I don't want to get involved, let's not" means less than the tone of voice, the look in the eye, or the accompanying gesture. The echo of what one means is not literally what one says, but could in nuance and situation (like Pan) be any or everything, depending on the shape of what's around, the shape of the line, the stanza, the situation. This shaping of words in their echo is shown in the tale. Narcissus, searching for his companions, cries, "Is anyone here?" "Here!" Echo responds. Though she has echoed Narcissus's very words, his literal meaning has been changed through her echo.

Later, as she attempts to approach Narcissus, he cries, "Hands off! Embrace me not! May I die before I give you power over me!" "I give you power over me," echoes Echo. So echo is not only an echo of something, but also a kind of response that completes the word to itself.

It seems to me that this deepening echo, or echo that completes the word to itself, is much of what aesthetic, and certainly psychological, understanding is all about. In psychotherapy it is important to notice what echoes how. Some things echo empty (like a Pinter play), some things echo overfull (like a heavily symbolic poem), some things echo flat then big (like melodrama), and some things echo not at all – like jargon, say, or interpretation ("I have an inferior feeling function, a mother complex, an Oedipal complex." Well, so what?). Jargon and explanation, because widely communicative and acceptable (a Hera language), bear little Echo.

Echo is really quite particular and articulate like the nooks and crannies of a cave, the undulations of a valley, the precise jagged points where rock emerges and recedes. These details, these precisions, make for Echo.

In the tale we are presented with some of these imagistic details. For example, when Echo sees Narcissus, she is "inflamed with love" (*flamma propiore calescit*). She does not "fall" in love, as one says (perhaps now, certainly twenty years ago). Nor is the image "turned on," as we might say now, as though one's love were a kind of mechanical device. No, Echo was inflamed. The image is burning. Ovid says:

> Now when Echo saw Narcissus wandering through the fields, she was inflamed with love and followed him by stealth; as when quick-burning sulphur, smeared round the tops of torches, catches fire from another fire brought near. Oh, how often does she long to approach him with alluring words and make soft prayers to him![73]

---

73 *Metamorphoses* 3.368–74.

Echo's passion is a quick, hot sulphur that nearness inflames. The attraction works through likening, so that the closer one gets to the similar, the quicker and hotter the fire. Like inflames, touches off, ignites like. So this is an attraction based not upon opposites, but upon similars. Though Narcissus resists, there is an essential similarity; Echo and Narcissus (subject and object, lover and beloved, pursuer and pursued) are of the same essential nature.

What does this similarity imply? In the realm of Echo and Narcissus, that every occurrence be a recurrence as well, every action a re-action. More personally it implies that what one echoes is very like oneself, and that within one's echoing is a kind of self.

Take mimicry as an example. Due to our notions of identity and separation, we tend to regard mimicry as a fairly low-level business. When a student mimics his teacher, or an analysand his analyst (in Zurich you could often tell whom a person worked with by his gestures and expressions), perhaps this mimicry is not just a lack of identity and originality. Perhaps psychologically this mimicking is a way of making flame, building heat.

As Echo imitates Narcissus (as subject imitates object, as lover imitates that which he loves, pursuer that which he pursues), a heat is created through this approaching nearness. The psychic situation gets tighter, more reflective, and the contrasts more subtle and telling. Imitation is a mode of creating and shaping psychic heat. The psyche is in this way an artist – a shaper, maker, a creator of beauty within itself.

But important to this shaping of heat is also the shape of surroundings. As Echo shapes, she is shaped by what's around her. This is contrary to Narcissus. Narcissus denies Echo and thus that contour of world upon which Echo is dependent in order to echo, in order to be.

Like all of us, Narcissus would like to keep things simple. And it's much simpler to think of one's self and identity and subjectivity as separate from the world of echoes – the shape of one's self and experience as different from the shape of surroundings.

Narcissus, we must remember, is self-enclosed and one. If anyone has "identity," Narcissus has it. Early on I made a jab at psychology for so having focused on identity. Indeed, now psychology is obsessed with narcissism. (Every professional conference you go to and every article you pick up have something to do with it.) The two, narcissism and identity, are not so different. Identity is just the nice word for it. Identity, self-continuity, self-intention, subjectivity – all this identity talk has a narcissistic underside. "How do you feel?" asks the kindly therapist. "Well, I feel – uh, angry," says the patient, thereby establishing his self-reflection, self-identity, and narcissistic strength.

Superficial Narcissus has to do with these self-statements, statements that detach themselves from the world of Echo. "I feel much better about myself." Narcissism patters through therapeutic awareness. Maybe we need this, and it is archetypal; but it's only part of an archetype. The rest has to do with Echo and her longing, not just Narcissus and his. Maybe the reason we have concentrated on Narcissus to the exclusion of Echo is that Echo's passion is much more difficult.

Echo's passion is painful; her longing is unrealizable. Echo's passion requires a distance, a space between her and her beloved. To be true to Echo, one must cultivate this distance that agonizes and yet is one's aesthetic passion. In other words, to develop the echo in one's narcissism one must achieve a certain painful distance in and by which this echo can sound.

What is this sense of distance? It is perhaps what Gaston Bachelard calls the "unreality function"; Walter Ong, "interior resonance"; T. S. Eliot, the "escape from personality"; and Gerard Hopkins, the "selfless self of self."

It is obvious that whatever we are after here is a commonplace in post-Romantic poetics. So, too, in the poetics of psyche – it would seem that for any work that depends on Echo, the cultivation of imaginative distancing is essential.

Let's return to the "I feel" example. One way to distance this feeling would be to specify who or what feels angry. By localizing the feeling, one gains a kind of precision within a particular image and context. The psychic imagination (as does the poetic) proceeds by means of differentiation.

By asking who, what (Henry Corbin's emphasis), by precise form in image, one creates a distance among psychic figures and breaks up "ego identity," that all-devouring "I." Within these spaces that mark distinct differences, echo can begin to sound (so that the distance becomes through Echo also a kind of nearness).

Of course, there are many other ways to create this distant nearness in therapy, and good therapists can do so, I think, instinctively. At least, in those rare moments when one is a good therapist, one is in touch with this sense of Echo. The point is not distance between analyst and analysand, but intrapsychic distance, distance *within* the psyche. It is not that the analyst must maintain distance by not seeing the analysand socially, withholding personal facts about himself, keeping his feelings separate, and so on. Rather it is that Echo's longing and suffering must in the work of the analysis be preserved. This sensitive cultivation of suffering is an art having more to do with echoing tones and moods within the psyche than with grand rules or analytic proscriptions.

Rafael López-Pedraza, that much-quoted, annoying, tricksterish sage (whom if he didn't exist, we'd have to invent), was good with what he called "very bad shape" persons. He'd take people out of hospitals who had been there most of their lives and teach them how to live alone and keep house for themselves. He'd instruct them in shopping at the market, washing dishes, ironing… The trick is that for him these mundane chores were full of echo. If someone had been ironing, he'd say, "Aha, you're ironing? Ironing, hum-uh, ironing!" Echo was there in the word, in the activity. He didn't interpret – "Your ironing is like flattening out your mother" or "Your ironing is because you were never allowed to iron as a child." Rather, he preserved the echo in the word and thus in the activity.

This echoing distance creates a space for beauty. And Echo's beauty implies not only the heat we mentioned earlier, but also suffering, affliction, sorrow. Echo's beauty is equally a suffering and a certain passivity. That is to say, it is a suffering of something beyond one's self-identified bounds or ego. It's related to the Latin *passio*, the Greek *pathos*. This passion is like a taste or touch all the more poignant because it isn't actual. Or a passion all the more precious because of the pain of its nonconsummation. Nothing in the myth of Echo and Narcissus gets fulfilled – there's no happy ending – at least not in any ordinary sense.

The focus of the myth is on unfulfilled passion (Echo for Narcissus and Narcissus for his reflection).

It's extraordinary how often in life or in dreams the unfulfilled is important. I mean, our natural longing is that things be consummated and be made fact – real – that we indeed end up with the person we long for, that strong attraction turns into physical, factual completion. Yet how often in life and in dreams this turns out to be not the point at all. I'm thinking of those dreams in which one is pushed away or rejected, as though, if you take the dream seriously, consummation is not what the psyche is about.

I remember a man in analysis who had dream after dream of women flirting with him, seducing him – brushing his cheek, letting him touch their breasts, touching his penis. But in each case, as he tried in the dream to move into actual love-making, these figures rebuffed him. It was as though the natural course was not the way, consummation not the point, but that each of these discrete attractions – the breast, the cheek, the longing – was important.

When this motif of unfulfilled or unrequited love is constellated, we should perhaps think less of the consummation desired and more of what is actually there, what is actually emphasized in the dream: breasts, cheek, touch – distinct sensuous details. In the tale of Echo and Narcissus, there is no consummation in any ordinary sense. But there is a kind of self-consummation in death, a consummation of the complex within itself.

Let us now look at Echo's death. According to Ovid, Echo's love feeds on the fact that she is rejected. Her love "grows on grief." It becomes greater because of the grief. And in this love grief, her body wastes away until "she becomes gaunt and wrinkled and all moisture fades from her body into air. Only her voice and her bones remain: then, only voice; for they say that her bones were turned to stone."

Echo's body becomes etiolated, a body of air. In a curious way, this drying through grief has resulted in another kind of substantiation. As Echo is lost to the air, she is in the air. It's no longer the concrete physical (Hera's real) that is real now, but the air that is real (and structured) – real with the power to echo. Echo in what's heard, in what happens, in events is real, and Echo's bones are given as the form, the structure, of that reality.

We have a lot to learn about the discrimination of Echo as bone and then stone, a lot of training of the ear in order to hear when beauty falls from the air. It's like hearing the echo of soul embodied. It's like hearing a voice in the nature of things – a knowledge in the stone of the bones.

VIII

Hamlet's Poisoned Ear

The Tragedy of Hamlet, Prince of Denmark has been called Shakespeare's most psychological play. Certainly it has fascinated the imagination of critics – including notables like Voltaire, Goethe, Samuel Johnson, Boswell, Coleridge, Charles Lamb, Shaw, T. S. Eliot, C. S. Lewis. More has been written on this play than on any other in the English language.

Interpretations of "Hamlet's problem" – his delay in avenging his father's murder – range widely. Goethe sees Hamlet as too sensitive, Shaw as too humane, and Coleridge as an intellectual, introspective personality suffering the problem of contemplation versus action. These romantic interpretations, which dominated the nineteenth century, generally view reflection and action as naturally opposed.

There is also a strand of moral criticism concerned with Hamlet's culpability. Some (like Samuel Johnson, G. Wilson Knight, Salvador de Madariaga) view him as cruel or inhuman or compelled to evil by the ghost who is the devil in disguise.

Other moral critics see Hamlet as essentially good or at least as morally concerned as the critics themselves. For them, his hesitation reflects his ethical nature, his moral need to determine whether the ghost is good or evil. Here the idea is that morality slows down action until good and evil are clearly determined – upon which, action is presumably swift and unfaltering.

Because of Shakespeare's development of Hamlet as a character, there has been much psychological interpretation. Lily Campbell sees

Hamlet as suffering a grief reaction from his father's death; Bradley speaks of Hamlet's melancholia. Ernest Jones, of course, spots the Oedipal complex. Hamlet cannot revenge his father's death, since Hamlet unconsciously wished his father dead. Whereas the Oedipal approach points up the ambivalence in Hamlet's feelings for his mother throughout the play, it does so at the expense of treating the play in terms of the psychological interpretation of another play, Oedipus Rex.

Let us spend a moment with this Freudian interpretation to see what it assumes about myth. Freudian psychology sees myth as universal and unitary (there is only one basic story relevant to the psyche of human beings). Myth is clear and unequivocal (behavior and works of the imagination can be shown to derive rationally from it). Myth is unalterable (one never gets out of the fundamental myth). Myth is a root reduction (many details and variations can be reduced to basic mechanisms).

This view of myth is appropriate for a psychology that seeks to be causal in method and parsimonious in explanation. It is also fitting that a psychology like this turn for its mythic model to Sophocles' Oedipus Rex, a play reflecting the Greek sense of clear design and unalterable fate.

But, say, we are engaged in another kind of psychology – an archetypal psychology that is relative and pluralistic, based on imagination (rather than explanation), a psychology that must constantly shift its point of view to avoid the literalism of any stance. Equivocating to evoke, breaking down to reveal, this psychological method has no fixed structure or clear systematic. A fitting mythic analogue for its process is Shakespeare's Hamlet, a drama supreme in evocative mystery and unsettling ambiguity.

*

The play begins with a ghost. A ghost who looks like the former king appears on three successive nights to the watchmen outside Elsinore castle. The reactions of the watchmen are various: they are dumbstruck; they think it a disguised presence, perhaps not the king as it seems; they think it mere fantasy needing approval by the senses or by scholarship; Marcellus and Bernardo challenge it with their spears; Horatio, skeptic and scholar, charges that it speak, but only on his conditions:

(1) if it has something good to say; (2) if it has knowledge of the country's fate, which, thus forewarned, Denmark might avoid; (3) if it has knowledge of buried treasure. It's little wonder that the ghost walks away.

Hamlet's treatment of the ghost is more phenomenological. He says he will call it as it seems, Hamlet, King, Father, Royal Dane; he confesses himself a fool, limited, ignorant of supernatural truths, so when the ghost beckons, he follows. The ghost takes him to a *removed ground*. This ground removed is separate from Hamlet's companions and the kinds of questions they have been asking. Removed ground is for them threatening; they fear suicide or madness. Hamlet accepts these possibilities and follows.

The ghost then speaks to him and reveals the circumstances of his death:

> ... *Sleeping within mine orchard,*
> *My custom always in the afternoon,*
> *Upon my secure hour thy uncle stole*
> *with juice of cursed hebenon in a vial,*
> *And in the porches of mine ears did pour*
> *The leperous distilment* ... [74]

Though it is commonly thought the king died from the poison of a serpent, that serpent is actually his brother Claudius, Hamlet's uncle, who has now married the queen and rules the kingdom. The ghost urges Hamlet to revenge this abomination. His parting words are *Remember me*. Hamlet promises he will and writes down what the ghost has said: *So, uncle, there you are. Now to the word: it is "Adieu, adieu, remember me." I have sworn't.* Note that Hamlet does not swear to revenge, but to remember.

Remembrance of the ghost is the key to Hamlet's behavior throughout the play. In this sense, the ghost is the supernatural motivating figure behind the action, much as the gods were in Greek drama. But there are important differences.

A ghost is not a god. A god in the Greek imagination presented itself unambiguously. When Apollo appeared to Orestes urging him to

---

74 Act I, Sc. 5.

revenge his father's murder, there was no question as to Apollo's reality, no need for approval by the senses or by scholarship. No one dared lay down conditions by which the god could speak. A god was a divine presence, a reality.

In Shakespeare's Elizabethan world, the gods have become "pagan" ambiguous presences (fairies, witches, or ghosts), vague half-truths, apparitions, whirling fancy, wild imaginings. What appears is no longer necessarily what is. Appearance is subject to perspective and interpretation. Man is the measure, and the mythic moment shifts to the eye of the beholder.

Gods become principles. Apollo or Zeus as protectors of kingship appear principled as divine right. Symbols, allusions, metaphors take over for the gods. When Hamlet says his father was like Hyperion to a satyr, he metaphorically evokes the solar god (Hyperion) through simile. The Apollo who backs Agamemnon is not a metaphor, but a presence; not a symbol of illumination, but an illuminating presence.

In Shakespeare's world the gods no longer directly protect and limit the imagination; they occur rather through its tropes, allusions, symbols, decorations. We have moved from god to symbol, from presence to principle, from divine figure to figure of speech.

But in any era divinity doth hedge a king,[75] as Claudius says. The murder of a king is a serious offense, an affront to the god or principle by which the "kingdom" (life itself, consciousness) is ordered. To lose that orienting lumination leaves one lost, if not ill. Hamlet says he is sick from the sun, having been too much in it. On one level, this sun allusion is an equivocation, sun and son. Hamlet is too much the son of a solar father who is now a ghost. To be the son of a ghost – that shadowy, vague consciousness – is indeed disorienting. How is one to respond to a luminary father who is an insubstantial half-presence? Greek heroes were sons of gods, not ghosts. For them, action, like the god, was unambivalent.

There is a moment of hesitation in the Orestia but an instructive one, I think. As Orestes is about to kill his mother, Clytemnestra, he falters

---

75 Act 4, Sc. 5.

and asks his companion, *What will I do, Pylades? – I dread to kill my mother!* Pylades answers, *What of the future? What of the Prophet God Apollo, the Delphic voice, the faith and oaths we swear? Make all mankind your enemy, not the gods.*[76]

With his priorities now in order, Orestes kills his mother. This horrifying action is divinely backed, so that to falter in it, as Pylades reminds, would be to dishonor the God of the oracle, the Apollo who directs Orestes' actions.

In *Hamlet* the sun is not directive, but destructive. Horatio speaks of *disasters in the sun*. The sun is *like a good kissing carrion*.[77]

Let her not walk i'th' sun, Hamlet warns Polonius, *conception is a blessing, but not as your daughter may conceive*.[78] On one level a dirty joke (conception punned into pregnancy), the joke also forebodes Ophelia's madness.

One must not walk innocently in direct sun, and Ophelia is a naive soul. She speaks simply, *Ay, my lord; No, my lord; My lord, I do not know.* Innocently she has received Hamlet's attentions and just as innocently betrays him to her father. As she passively undervalues herself, she also naively overvalues her importance, assuming Hamlet's antic behavior proof of his love for her, a love so excessive it has driven him quite mad. To Ophelia's simplicity (or from a simplistic point of view), Hamlet appears mad (*O what a noble mind is here o'erthrown!*[79]). But Ophelia is the one who becomes so. In her madness, *thought and affliction, passion, hell itself, / She turns to favour and to prettiness.*[80] Ophelia drowns attempting to attach flowers to a hoar-leafed, overhanging willow, to prettify the funerary tree.

Hamlet does not drown in his vision nor is it pretty. His walk in the sun is to defile the material world. He views matter as *rank, gross, dead,* like a dead dog breeding maggots. The world is *an unweeded garden, a sterile promontory.* Men are *pictures or mere beasts.* His mother lives in *rank sweat, stewed in corruption* in a *nasty sty.* Hamlet assaults the sensual

---

76 *The Oresteia* 899ff. (trans. R. Fagles).
77 Act 2, Sc. 2.
78 Ibid.
79 Act 3, Sc. 1.
80 Act 4, Sc. 5.

world with abusive metaphors. Whereas Ophelia attempts to ignore a rotten Denmark or to reconstitute it through pretty songs, Hamlet joins with and aids its breakdown with a verbal destructiveness that is at once alchemical – mortifying and putrefying the material. His action is through words – words that require a certain kind of ear.

★

The play, as you will remember, begins with hearing. The sentry post outside the castle is in darkness when the curtain opens.

Nothing can be seen, only heard. *Who's there?* are the opening words, which set the tone in auditory suspiciousness. Coleridge remarks on the detailed attunement of the ear evoked in this first scene in which *not a mouse is stirring*. One is asked to hear very finely.

Indeed hearing (and overhearing) is a theme throughout. When Hamlet meets the ghost, the ghost instructs, *Pity me not, but lend thy serious hearing.* Hamlet responds, *Speak, I am bound to hear.* Ghost: *List, Hamlet, list, O list!* [81] The first act alone has twenty references to hearing.

The ear is a central image. The king was murdered by being poisoned in the ear. So not only is the ghost a vague half-presence, but also his ear is tainted. This tainting of the ear is like the Fall – the orchard is the original garden; Claudius is called *the serpent* – bringing a mythical overtone of inevitability. Original, innocent hearing must fail; the ear is inevitably poisoned; knowledge gained through its loss.

So far I have used the Greeks to say that what was lost was like the loss of gods. I have contrasted the Greek with Hamlet's world in which things are no longer as they seem (appearance split from reality, principle and symbol from what they represent).

But this contrast is ever-present. For the Greek world is original, pure, basic, direct; Hamlet's world, complicated, corrupt, indirect. One imagines an original purity, which is then corrupted. Poisoning is an image of this corruption. But poison (*pharmakon*) is also medicine. Poison cures homeopathically, as like cures like.

---

81 Act I, Sc. 5.

The king's ear has been corrupted from an original purity. But the curative medicine, the *pharmakon* for this corruption, is further corruption. The cure of the tainted ear is to taint it yet again. Hamlet's acrimonious activity attempts a cure through hearing and language – multiple meanings, metaphors, ironies. Hamlet, as the son of a ghost with a poisoned ear, is cursed to torture and be tortured through language.

But effective irony requires anchor – vertical connection with some god, principle, tradition – an axis that limits its corruptive movement. In *Hamlet* the ghost, ambiguous though he is, makes for that vertical, more-than-human connection.

There's the puzzling scene where Hamlet asks his companions of the watch not to tell anyone of the ghost. Though they assure him they would not, he wants them to swear officially upon his sword. Then each time as Hamlet has his sword extended and they are about to make the oath, the ghost intones *Swear* from beneath the stage. Hamlet then shifts to another place, gathers everyone; just as they have their hands on his sword: *Swear*, the ghost intones. Four times this occurs, each time Hamlet shifting ground, before finally submitting to an oath with the ghostly *Swear* beneath it.

This is strange, since a moment earlier Hamlet had promised the ghost he would remember, that he was *bound to hear*, yet now we find him shifting position around the stage as though to elude that to which he is bound, to make an oath on his sword alone, without the god. But the ghost insists on a deeper, vertical binding and limitation.

Critics have pointed to the giddiness and superficiality of Hamlet's behavior in this scene to show how the meeting with the ghost has been too much. Indeed, Hamlet attempts to make light of the connection: *Ah ha, boy, sayst thou so? Art thou there, truepenny? ... Well said, old mole ... Once more remove, good friends.* [82] Hamlet's triviality, giddiness, superficiality – the more *removed ground* here become a horizontal defense, shifting ground to evade – nevertheless attest to the seriousness of Hamlet's task. To connect to the ghost deeply, as a divine presence beneath him-

---

self, his actions, his oaths, is a responsibility he may well wish to avoid. Vertical axis to the Underworld is dangerous indeed.

It is said that Shakespeare himself played the part of the ghost in the original production. So we might make allusion as well to ghost as writer, as author, perhaps "divine author." On many levels, something demands of Hamlet a deeper connection to what he is about. The poisoning work he is to do must serve the ghost beneath himself.

Hamlet serves through language. He is unabashedly literary. Words carry much of the action of the drama. Hamlet's action with the ghost, *as* we remember, was not to challenge it, as did Horatio, or to take up arms against it, like Marcellus and Bernardo, but – following it to a ground removed – to write down what the ghost has said, creating remembrance as a written text.

Even at the simplest level of plot, the written word plays a notable role. There is Hamlet's letter to Ophelia, which she shows to her father, which then forms the subplot (the erroneous belief that Hamlet's madness is due to his love for her, of which his letter is proof). There is the scene where Hamlet, reading from a book, uses the text as pretext for his mockery of Polonius. Then there is that turning point, Hamlet's "abridgement," the play within the play he writes to *catch the conscience of the King*. There is Claudius's letter sent with Rosencrantz and Guildenstern to England ordering Hamlet's death. There is Hamlet's letter, replacing that letter, ordering the deaths of Rosencrantz and Guildenstern. There is Hamlet's letter to Horatio telling of the former two letters and of a crucial turn of events occurring offstage, namely, Hamlet having been captured by pirates, the pirates' taking pity on him, and of his intended return to Denmark. One can tell the whole story through letters.

But words are also part of the sickness of the kingdom. *Words, words, words,* reports Hamlet with some justification.[83] *More matter with less art,* Gertrude chides.[84] Denmark is ill with the flourishes of empty courtly talk. It is difficult to distinguish between deed and painted word.

---

83 Act 2, Sc. 2.
84 Ibid.

Since the ear is tainted and, with the ear, language, there is a verbal excess without bounds or attunement. Osric, the courtier, exemplifies this extravagant abuse of language, for instance, when he tells Hamlet of Laertes' arrival:

> Osric   *Sir, here is newly come to court Laertes, believe me, an absolute gentleman, full of most excellent differences, of very soft society and great showing. Indeed, to speak feelingly of him, he is the card or calendar of gentry, for you shall find in him the continent of what part a gentleman would see.*

Hamlet mocks Osric by responding with some masterly satirical bit of his own mixed metaphor:

> Hamlet   *Sir, his definement suffers no perdition in you, though, I know, to divide him inventorially would dizzy th' arithmetic of memory, and yet but yaw neither in respect of his quick sail. But in the verity of extolment, I take him to be a soul of great article, and his infusion of such dearth and rareness as, to make true diction of him, his semblance is his mirror, and who else would trace him, his umbrage, nothing more.*
>
> Osric   *Your lordship speaks most infallibly of him.*
>
> Hamlet   *The concernancy, sir? Why do we wrap the gentleman in our more rawer breath?*
>
> Horatio   *Is't not possible to understand in another tongue? You will to't, sir, rarely.*
>
> Hamlet   *What imports the nomination of this gentleman?*
>
> Osric   *Of Laertes?*
>
> Horatio   *His purse is empty already; all's golden words are spent.* [85]

Hamlet's mockery of Osric's exaggerated speech undoes Osric completely. (He finally forgets what he's talking about.) Without his *golden words* he is at a loss. Language gone astray like Osric's is the symptom of a corrupted ear, an ear no longer in tune with what it is about, no longer sensing the irony, the insubstantiality of the ghost in itself. (The sickness

---

[85] Act. 5, Sc. 2.

is not knowing the ghost, not hearing its echoing insubstantiality in language, and so being unable to work it, to make something of it.)

Hamlet also mocks Polonius, Ophelia's father. Polonius's language, though frivolous, also has the quality of common sense or custom – at its best (as in the scene with Laertes), a certain "conventional wisdom." We like much of what Polonius says. In fact, many of the lines we remember from the play were actually spoken by him: *By indirections find directions out; Neither a borrower nor a lender be; To thine own self be true, | And it must follow, as the night the day, | Thou canst not then be false to any man; Take each man's censure, but reserve thy judgment.* And on and on: *Be thou familiar but by no means vulgar ...* We enjoy these precepts because we recognize them – they are conventional, and we are amused by their everyday validity.

But Hamlet finds Polonius annoying, calls him a *tedious old fool*, a *wretched, rash, intruding fool*, a *foolish prating knave*. Although Polonius is a bit foolish, he is not unkind or intentionally evil, and he is affectionately tolerated by the court (as he most probably also was when Hamlet's father was king). Hamlet's hatred for Polonius really has to do with the way he talks. Conventional wisdom, cliché, customary platitudes are to Hamlet's ear unforgivable.

In the first act, Hamlet promised the ghost to wipe from mind *all trivial fond records, | All saws of books, all forms ... | That youth and observation copied there.* [86] Hamlet vowed not to hear, not to register or remember, the copied or conventional.

Whereas Polonius says to *give every man thine ear but few thy voice*, Hamlet gives every man his voice, but is very selective about his ear. Mimicked platitudes must be destroyed before hearing can hear reflectively. Hamlet must first kill the Polonius hidden behind the arras before his mother can reflect her sins. Conventional wisdom, though a *dear old man*, as Claudius calls him, is also *a rat*, as Hamlet calls him, that must be thrust right through.

Hamlet's language is unmistakably individual, improvisational, skilled, and complex. It is never merely verbose, decorative, clichéd, or

---

86 Act i, Sc. 5.

beside the point. Indeed, he disapproves of players who *speak more than is set down for them*. An actor must be as loyal to his text or playwright as is Hamlet to his ghost. And at this point Hamlet is loyal. No longer is he wandering around the stage to avoid the undertone, the supposition, the vertical axis that sounds beneath.

A characteristic of Hamlet's speech is his use of repetition: *I humbly thank you, well, well, well; Words, words, words; Mother, mother, mother!; ... except my life, my life, my life.* Repetition in threes expresses an apotropaic rhythmic power for Hamlet. One could argue that words for him are sometimes less important than what he does with them; that is, he uses words to conjure something intangible and then to make something through language of that intangibility. He works the ghost through words.

For example, let's take the scene where Hamlet is "reading" and Polonius approaches (insinuating himself to espy the reasons for Hamlet's madness):

> Polonius   *... What do you read, my lord?*
> Hamlet   *Words, words, words.*
> Polonius   *What is the matter, my lord?*
> Hamlet   *Between who?*
> Polonius   *I mean the matter you read, my lord.* [87]

Hamlet mocks Polonius's superficial *What do you read?* (a ruse to open conversation) with an irrelevant and more superficial response: *Words, words, words.* This drop of poison (like-cures-like, superficial-superficial) creates an irony and an echo. *Words, words, words* also implies "words like yours, Polonius, are empty" and "words is all there is." *What is the matter, my lord?* Hamlet again poisons through a pun on the word "matter." *Between who? I mean, the matter you read, my lord.* Hamlet's equivocation on "matter" takes the most superficial sense (like "what is the matter?") and places it between (*Between who?*) relationally. Thus Hamlet both mocks the matter of personal relationships and yet places matter as a realm between. The irony is at least fivefold: the double meaning of matter, matter misunderstood, trivialized by him who is least trivial in his

87 Act 2, Sc. 2.

concern with it, placed in relation between (in a world where relationship is lacking), and then the final irony: this evidently matters.

Hamlet's double entendres, puns, equivocations create the ghost. By
poisoning what is said, he creates a space within which words *because* of
their duplicity (multiplicity) have meaning. To serve the ghost, to make
something of it, to remember it, there must be a further poisoning.
Reality is equivocal, so the mode is not to go along naively (Ophelia)
or with empty words (Osric) or custom (Polonius) but to craft the space
between meanings. The method of this madness is destructive: it must
poison the superficial to create on another level.

Another tool of the work is reversal. Hamlet compulsively reverses
whatever is. If someone speaks to him with apparent directness, as does
Polonius when he asks what Hamlet is reading, Hamlet responds indirectly in order to upset the mode in which the question was asked. But when
indirection goes too far, so that it is no longer imaginatively productive,
no longer creating anything, Hamlet reverses the process and becomes
pointedly direct. We see this with Osric. After Hamlet has thoroughly
mocked Osric's exaggerated description of Laertes, he says pointedly,

> *What imports the nomination of this gentleman?*
> Osric   *Of Laertes?*
> [...]
> Hamlet   *Of him, sir.*

Then again:

> *What's his weapon?*[88]

Hamlet is equally direct with Rosencrantz and Guildenstern: *Were
you not sent for? ... I know the good King and Queen have sent for you.*

He counters the indirect with the direct and the direct with the indirect. The point is always to create something by destroying the first
level of what is said.

We find a touching example of this equivocation when Hamlet ad-
mits to Ophelia:

----

88 Act 5, Sc.2.

Hamlet	*I did love you once.*
Ophelia	*Indeed, my lord, you made me believe so.*
Hamlet	*You should not have believed me ... I loved you not.* [89]

Here Hamlet begins directly, *I did love you once*, but then when Ophelia responds in kind (*Indeed ... you made me believe so*), he reverses himself. It's as though he must avoid the collusion of agreement between feelings. It is not that Hamlet did or did not love, but both. He did and he did not. Ambiguity, like the ghost, is the true emotion, and honest speaking must honor that.

But now how is one to act in this kind of world, a world that undoes what is and is what is not. I have maintained that Hamlet's action occurs primarily through language, but what of physical action – that action with which Hamlet himself and certainly most critics of the play are concerned.

One of the gravediggers says, *an act hath three branches; it is to act, to do, and to perform.* [90] This is meant to be a parody of legal hair-splitting, but let's drop a bit of poison and take it for what it is not. After all, they are gravediggers whose wisdom is very likely to be vertically anchored.

Let us call the first kind of action the action of the play itself. Classically, a tragedy is supposed to show one complete, inevitable, and necessary action. Usually the main character is fully heroic at the beginning; then there is a reversal, recognition, and fall. But here everything is backwards. Hamlet is more "fallen" in the beginning than he is at the end; there are reversals and recognitions throughout; the plot, rather than "necessary" and "inevitable," moves by way of circumstance and accident.

Rosencrantz and Guildenstern just happen to meet the players on the road and so invite them to the court; Hamlet accidentally kills Polonius; the ship taking him to England just happens to be attacked by pirates who, for some unexplained reason, happen to take pity on him; Hamlet and Horatio by coincidence return to Denmark through the graveyard where, it just so happens, Ophelia is being buried; Gertrude accidentally

---

89 Act 3, Sc. 1.
90 Act 5, Sc. 1.

drinks from the wrong cup; swords are accidentally switched; as all four are dead or dying Fortinbras happens to come through Denmark just as Hamlet has announced his dying vote.

This mood of happenstance or accident attests to the kind of action being performed. One cannot say the play is flawed on that basis or an artistic "miscarriage" or "failure" (as Robertson and Eliot contend); rather, it is a drama in a universe without gods, where the motivating figure is a poisoned ghost. To assume another situation would be to ignore the taint behind it all and to demand another play.

The second kind of action: to do (act as intention or will). Critics who think in terms of willed intention – Hamlet should have willed to do otherwise, should have made a choice whether to be or not to be – these kinds of interpretations are the furthest from what I've been trying to do, i.e., a psychological reading that does not separate intention from what appears or will from what happens. The play is its "objective correlative."

The play's the thing [91] brings us to the third kind of action, the action I think Hamlet is about: act as to perform. Hamlet learns to act by becoming like a performer, a player whose will is turned over to something other – a text, the necessities of script, or providence.

This opening to something other was effected through Hamlet's work with language. Reversals, contradictions, ambivalences served to unhinge identities and loosen fixity, creating the ghost as an imaginative entity, a half-presence between. In this place between, action becomes possible as a further imagining.

This action is not an "acting out" of one or another aspect of the ghost – real or imagined, heroic or reflective – but a movement with imagination in its entirety. Hamlet becomes as a player within a larger realm, upon a world stage. The "conscience" that the play catches is Hamlet's own. As the poisoned ear becomes a visibly concrete image in the play, concrete enactment follows upon it. The world is a play and the concrete no longer simply a literal behavior, but through the play the concrete world becomes an extension of the imagination. This move-

91 Act. 2, Sc. 2.

ment from literal to imaginal reality is the only way Hamlet can enter into action. The imagination releases him to perform. There are no fixed rules for this enacting. Look at Hamlet's "rules": he warns the players against *dumb shows*, pantomimes, yet he writes a dumb show for the king; he warns against over-dramatization, speaking more than is set down, yet he himself elaborates and dramatizes. The principles Hamlet gives for performance are contradicted in his behavior. But these contradictions are the very nature of his activity. Hamlet can act only if the ambiguity of the ghost is built into the action, only if the action be imaginative as well.

This imaginative action cannot be fixed as rule. It exists in the interim between old rule and new – old gods, old words, old king, and the ordering of the new. This midzone, though psychologically concrete, cannot be established as a kingdom. It makes way for Fortinbras's new kingdom, but it cannot exist within it.

At the conclusion of the play, we learn the new regime will be in fact little different from the old, *armed at all points exactly, cap-à-pie*. Young Fortinbras who inherits the kingdom is headstrong and military (his name means literally "strong-in-arm"). *With divine ambition puffed*, Fortinbras finds honor through *quarrel in a straw* and conquers lands *that hath in it no profit but the name.* [92] Perhaps name is profit enough, and the grounds, grounds for new order. Hamlet gives his vote to the hope and then dies. Hamlet must die to the new establishment so that the ghost remain a ghost, the half-presence of ambiguity that is the play and that keeps *Hamlet* alive. Kingdoms come and go, but the name that lasts is the play's to which Hamlet gave his and through which he continues to exist.

Hamlet lingers on as story. He continues to exist in the fantasy of any psyche loyal to a ghost, subversive to fixity. But it makes a difference who tells the story. With Horatio's story we anticipate a tale of external actions, approved by the senses and by scholarship, told with balanced reason and good judgment. I doubt this is the whole story or the real action. The whole story is the story of the imagination; the real action is

---

92 Act 4, Sc. 4.

that imagining. Hamlet remains as a ghost in our Western imagination, a haunting presence bound to equivocate, tied to ambiguity, released into activity through the action of language.

A *"Psychological" Postscript*

I was asked, after delivering this paper as a talk, what it has to do with psychology. For me it is psychology – though perhaps how this is so needs some spelling out. I had found myself weary of saying "psychologically" or "this is like" and then going on to make a "psychological" translation – which in the case of Hamlet seemed a particularly heavy-handed undertaking. But let me offer at this point a few notes on the ghost, upon which my view of Hamlet's "psychology" turns.

The ghost is an imaginal presence like a hallucination or a vision or a dream image or just some vague visibility that persists. The reactions of the watchmen are like those of everyman in the face of illusion. Unable to engage the presence, they consider it a disguise as Freud regarded dream images disguises for something thought to be more basic than the illusion itself: an illusion must be sensible or at least make sense. Like Horatio one demands that the illusion yield to reasonable concerns. We will hear the image if it is beneficial to do so or if the hearing brings prophetic knowledge or carries secret treasure.

Hamlet acquiesces to another kind of awareness. He moves to a ground apart. Just that shift-aside gives an image of psychological remove, which then allows the ghost to speak. This shift tunes the ear to nuance, metaphor, double meanings, irony and so on, as it destroys naive, commonplace, and platitudinous talk.

This ear, however, must be vertically attuned. If an ear to language destroys, it must remember that for the sake of which it is destroying – and this is why, incidentally, I think the ghost reappears to Hamlet in the scene with Gertrude. He gets carried away with his destructive language, so that a recollection of what he is about is again necessary; he must rebind with the "spirit" beneath his activity.

This vertical binding is a requirement, if hearing is not to be sense-lessly destructive or just skittish and fanciful, an associative game-playing across surfaces. If hearing is to be "psychological," it must be bound to some principle or purpose beneath itself. It must be anchored and circumscribed.

In archetypal psychology we have termed this circumscription "sticking to the image." Wishing not to abuse the psyche but to deepen within it, we have limited our work to "the image." But what is the image? If it be based on a ghost, then image is not confined to configurations in dreams, but might appear also as the ghost within an emotion, a situation, a verbal or physical exchange, an entire life. The ghost is the scope limiting and the *spiritus rector* defining the work. To sense this ghost and to create with it form the art of psychological work.

The psychological art is ghostly, based on a ghost. It is not founded by fiat as a kingdom or system. Its real limitation is given not by a conceptual scheme from above, no matter how revealing or supposedly "psychological." Rather, the work is secured by a half-visible presence, a deeper ground with darker demands.

Let us beware of kingdoms, systems, and structures. We may make way for them (as Hamlet makes way for Fortinbras), but let us then be on about our ghostly work, a work bound less to kingdom and rule than to that grounding in an intangible presence. If "the psychological" be anything at all, it is just this making, re-making activity, which is at once a remembering in service of the ghost.

IX

Stopping: A Mode of Animation

Psychological writing is a subjective confession, as Jung once noted. Let me quickly confess two fascinations, nay obsessions, behind this paper. One is an ingrained, incurable perversity, a compulsive fascination of mine with everything odd and pathological and twisted, especially the blocked, stuck, immovable regions of the psyche – the guy who can't come out of the corner, the catatonic with "waxlike flexibility," the mute child; symptoms like writer's block, stage fright, immobile depressions – as well as the blocked, stopped, stuck behaviors in all of us that don't move no matter how we try. *What is the psyche doing in these stoppings?*

Another fascination I have is myth. It has always seemed to me that myth isn't so much stories about the development of history, civilization, and consciousness as it is images of things eternal, things that repeat or perhaps have nothing to do with time at all – rather more a "gift of life meanings," as Robert Duncan has said. [93]

To indulge these two fascinations, I'd like to circle a myth usually called the Perseus tale. This myth satisfies my craving for pathology, since it contains sufficiently contorted and gruesome imagery: blood, murder, prison, incest, and the Medusa who stops you in your tracks and turns you to stone.

---

93 R. Duncan, *The Truth and Life of Myth: An Essay in Essential Autobiography* (Fremont, Mich.: The Sumac Press, 1968), 8.

Further, it seems a myth about stopping, about the stopping nature of myth – that myth has to do with static, eternal realities. It is a myth about myth in the same way that certain poems are about the making of poems, novels about novels.

And so my method will look at this myth in a way that stops it. This stopping feels disruptive, since it cripples the narrative force that would carry us along in a way that's more fun. Narrative arouses curiosity – what happens next, and then, and then? It feels as though something is *going* somewhere. Were we to read this myth as narrative, we'd get a wonderfully heroic tale – more a fairy tale than a myth. [94] We would get the rags-to-riches story of a young man who overcomes the circumstances of his birth (he's born in prison), defeats all obstacles, butchers the monster, redeems his mother, rescues and marries the beautiful maiden ...

But I don't want to do that. What I want instead is to stop that story prepense, deliberately by staying with some of its moments – its images or complexes – and then see what mode of animation, if any, occurs.

As a first image let's take Danae, Perseus's mother. Danae is locked in a cell by her father Acrisius, because it has been prophesied that she will give birth to a son, and that son will be her father's bane. The imprisoned Danae has been painted by many – Rembrandt, Primatticcio, Correggio, Titian; the most striking image is Titian's in which the fleshy maiden lounges seductively, receiving the shower of gold from Zeus into her luscious lap. Most prefer this opulent story of Perseus's birth, this immaculate conception, golden, raining down from the heavens. Surely it's the way a hero, a redeemer, ought to be conceived.

But there is another version in which Danae is seduced and impregnated by her uncle, her father's brother. We need to gather some background about this uncle. In fact, we need to go back before the uncle because the entire ancestry gives a certain basis to the pathology in the myth as a whole.

---

94 Cf. the distinction made by D. Miller in "Fairy Tale or Myth?" *Spring* 1976: *An Annual of Archetypal Psychology and Jungian Thought*, 157–64.

The primal ancestors of the Danaoi are twin brothers who hate each other. One brother sires fifty sons, the other fifty daughters. The daughters are strong Amazonic types, ferociously loyal to their father who is called "the wolf." When finally the daughters must marry the fifty sons (a massive group incest), forty-nine kill their young grooms on the wedding night. The fiftieth inadvertently betrays her father and sisters by falling in love with her victim. Although she is locked up and punished, her accident ensures that the family line and the myth, the mythic, are perpetuated. Myth depends on such accidents of fertility, accidents that stop myth's natural self-absorption, self-consumption, by a just as mythic collapse into unexpected generativity.

The next complication of this myth involves Danae's father Acrisius and her uncle Proitos – again twin brothers who hate each other so fundamentally that they try to kill each other while still in the fundament of their mother's womb. So within the familial womb itself there is bloody conflict. They are brothers in hatred; hatred is the family fraternity.

As adults, the brothers wage battle over the kingship of Argos. During the course of this battle a round shield is invented – the first shield of circular shape – as though inclusive of the warring opposites, a shield that protects by including all aspects of the family antipathy in an unbroken line.

But, of course, these wholeness constructions never quite work. Diagrammatic schemata and symbolic conceptions fail to wrap up the nature of myth, which no more than nature indulges in perfect circles. Symbolics can hardly shield us from the internal ancestral format, the deep pathologies in myth, and the eruptions, interruptions into the myth's attempts at its own solutions.

For example, this uncle then has three daughters and a son (four – again a symbolic number of wholeness). Symbolically, one would expect these four to round things off and settle the family pattern, but instead all four in different ways get driven mad and torn to bits.

But back to Danae. She and her uncle (whom the father hates) commit incest. I'm rather attracted to this incestuous version of Perseus's paternity, since incest is in keeping with the tangled emotionality of the family background: passion, hatred, murder, nature turned against itself, raging in the womb, dismemberment.

Incest works here because it brings a self-fertilization within the family of the family mess; the perverse circularity of incest makes for compounding, compacting the family horror. Within all this passionate hatred there is as well an incestuous self-fertilization, thickening the myth by turning it back into itself. It becomes ingrown. And how fertile this myth of myths. As Joseph Fontenrose has shown, [95] there are all but five of forty-three possible mythemes in the Perseus tale, none of which can claim priority as the earliest to make the rest derivative or secondary. This myth keeps generating new varieties of itself. It is a shower of gold, a fertile incest.

Another incestuous myth – Persephone captured by her father's brother Hades – is equally mysterious and equally fertile. And both Perseus and Persephone bear that prefix *perthou* (destroyer, ravager). Again a violent sort of pathology seems essential to the deepest sustaining mysteries that give meaning to human life. In the Persephone image it is Gaia, the very bowels of the Earth, who abets Hades's rape, and therefore insists on incest. As Freud and Jung saw, incest must be a universal complex; Gaia and Hades ordain it.

And if we carry this a step further, then incest appears in myths not just to make myths myths, make them superhuman, but to make the myths themselves. Myths demand the incest motif within them to show their own incestuous generation. Mythical consciousness is an incestuous consciousness which is allowed to mythical beings (like Pharaohs) and essential to *initiation into mythical thinking* as at Eleusis or in the alchemical model of individuation.

Incest, too, is an image of stopping, for it stops the normal exogamous course of events by inverting, fertilizing something back into itself. As the family blood, the complex, in a myth thickens and gathers weight, myth becomes mythic. Myth is incest. It's like poetry (*Dichtung, dicht* = thick, dense). It's dirty – the tales are terrible! One always wants

---

95 J. Fontenrose, *Python: A Study of Delphic Myth and its Origins* (New York: Biblo & Tannen, 1974).

to apologize for myth. It's not *logos*. It's not moral. It's not even Eros! So difficult to explicate, articulate, to draw out exogamously into the world or in a paper like this. The incest in it, the complex in it, resists, keeps it bound in a tight internal knot, inside its own family, its own thickness.

But incest is also like prison – the prison of shame, of secrecy. How often incest images show the pair in castles, islands, walled gardens, secret rooms. So, too, Danae is imprisoned by her father in a subterranean tomb under the palace.

Acrisius had wanted a son to carry on the family line. He had wanted to *extend* the family. We have already seen how this family myth-and-complex (the nature of myth and complex) is not to extend normally, exogamously outward, but to circle back into its own blood, as this discussion circles.

The oracle at Delphi tells Acrisius that he will not have a son. Normal movement into the world is not possible and, worse, his daughter will have a son who will defeat him. Faced with this prospect, the old man locks up his life (his *anima*); rigidifies, establishes, fixes his dark cellars of imagination into a dungeon of repression; and puts the soul down there. And when the daughter is locked in fixed constructs, the mythic potential of the psyche is locked and fixed as well. (Then indeed we get formulas, fixed symbolic meanings, allegories.)

*

So the daughter is locked in a tomb under the palace, and no seed, nothing fertile can get to her. Again the image is incestuous. Since the chamber is beneath the father's palace, it's like trying to keep the threatening thing, the *anima*, under oneself. It's keeping imperiously on top of it, above what's threatening. This is incest in a neurotic, superficial sense. Rather than connecting with *mythic* depths, this defensive binding keeps one on top of one's daughter – so that thought or work or emotions stay up, on the surface, superficial, and/or are imprisoned underneath. (It's like living in a duplex or split-level – you're walking around up on top while your daughter lies locked below.)

In the tale despite (or perhaps because of) all this suppression, fertilization occurs. It's like the return of the repressed or the fertility in the repressed. This is like gold. There's a shower of gold in the woman's lap, which lap grows in potentiality. She is now in confinement, as we used to call it. So again we have an image of stopping. Her pregnancy is her confinement; her confinement is her pregnancy. Within the prison of this cell, something germinates.

Imprisoning is crucial to a certain kind of new movement, again what we might call mythic movement. It is not your ordinary imprisonment, low-country imprisonment – just being bottled up, walled in, guarded, and oppressed. These conditions need to be imagined mythically, experienced incestuously, as if when one is in this low dungeon, there is something secret going on in the belly, that fantasies – not my enemies, my parents, my husband, or my fate – are confining me, that I am being held here by mythic events. Then this incestuous sense of generation going on within the confinement, the imprisoning, becomes a mode of self-fertilizing. So we do need the no-no's of rigidities, the impossible stone walls we cannot escape from or even see out of, in order to become aware that we are germinating mythic realities within ourselves.

Within this seclusion Perseus is born. As a child he sits playing happily with a golden ball. He can play with the mythic world as a golden ball because he is a child of incest, a child of the imagination. For him prison is like a little paradise. He's having a ball and, you know, for C. G. Jung the ball – particularly a golden ball – is a symbol of the Self. So Perseus is playing with himself. He's playing with himself until the ball rolls out of reach, and he loses himself. He cries out.

In this narcissistic image, paradisaical and self-enclosed, everything is fine – and silly and useless – until one's play with oneself rolls out of bounds, beyond one's own reach. Then like Narcissus, one cannot but tumble down into the depths or, as with Perseus, one suddenly finds the self extending out beyond one's self. It's like the world gets important because the self is out there too, and then you get frightened and scream out. It's like the complex cures itself. You lose yourself and then scream out, call out into the world – and then indeed you're out.

Acrisius hears this cry – it was probably meant for him – and throws them out of their containment, expels them from prison. So you see, the symptom "crying out," the unintended slip, makes the thing occur. Crying out takes them out.

The mother and child now appear in a box, a closed chest cast out to sea. Again we have an image of imprisonment: this time imprisoned in being adrift. Even though the prison under the palace, being imprisoned by the old king, was constricting and uncomfortable, nonetheless it *was* a sort of containment. You knew where you were. The walls were there, the boundaries fixed. But now those supports have all disappeared, and one is adrift.

Drifting is a terrible kind of imprisonment, like an Antonioni movie. One is out in the world but without ground; exposed to the elements but in a box, closed up. Adrift and yet isolated, cut off.

There are a number of ways for this floating imprisonment to end. You may get washed up on the shore of some solid reality, or smashed on a rock and opened, or maybe swallowed by a fish and carried east in the belly of some vague, oceanic intention – or again, one may be stopped more gently, in the bulrushes, caught up in the arms of a maiden.

But here, in this myth, the drifting ends in a net. A fisherman, Dictys (whose name means "net man"), sees the floating box and, being an imaginative fisherman, construes it as something wondrous – a magnificent sea monster *or* a god – so he nets and hauls it to shore. He's a fisherman with imaginative sight (mythic sight). He sees monsters and gods.

Just as Perseus floating with his mother in a little box on the wide sea appears in the same image as Dictys the fisherman, so, too, do floating and fishing occur in the same experience. When introspections are all boxed in, horizons limited by a low ceiling and walls of woodenness, then we are also fishing. How did this happen, what's going on, why am I so trapped? one asks, casting around for reasons, explanations, causes, while at the same time narrowed into oneself.

In this case, only a big net works. Only a vision that *sees* wondrously – gods and monsters – can rescue the smallness of mind that goes with introspection. Drifting does not have to be met with rational, "sensible perceptions of reality," as it or they are called.

Drifting is better arrested and landed by overperceiving, by perceiving the fantastical. When we let our fisherman pay out his mythical, animated imagination, then we are at once free of the box. When we can be imaginatively perceived, we can be landed. There are some good images for this art of perception in the myth, one of which occurs in the scene with the Graiae.

These are three sisters – daughters of Phorkys, the old man of the sea. The name Phorkys is the masculine form of Phorcis, that early mother-sow goddess. So Phorkys roots down into those deepest, earliest mysteries of the Earth. The Graiae, daughters of a pig-man, are pig-women. They have the pig in their background.

But the three sisters don't seem to show it. They are described as fair-faced and swanlike (that graceful bird of death). They have been gray-haired since birth, and their names (Enyo, Penphredo, and Dirno) mean warlike, wasp, and terrible. There is something fair about them (attractive), yet at the same time terrible and death-dealing in that very attractiveness. Perhaps this *terrible beauty* is one way of stating the deepest mysteries of the Earth, reminding of their father Phorkys and the sow-goddess who devours corpses and who also is associated with Hades (one of whose names is Orcus, again like hog).

So in this image of the Graiae we've got Hades, hog, the devouring of corpses, and a certain deathly, swanlike beauty, young and old together, forever gray-haired. Mythologically, psychologically, they are very archaic, very basic, deep goddesses (much older, for example, than the Olympians). They exist where death has beauty and beauty death, where pigs and swans concur. Their territory is a borderland between east and west, a place of darkness where the light sets and from which it has its beginning, a nowhere zone at the edge, the border of forests and rocks. The place is called the "land of rock-roses" – where the ephemeral delicacy of a rose is a rock, and a rock promises this ephemeral delicacy. The animate and inanimate are in this realm one and the same. Rock is rose and rose is rock. The most delicate, the most substantial.

Now these sisters have a single eye they pass around and share. According to one story, this is a magical eye that enables them to comprehend the tree alphabet in the forest that borders here. And their one tooth (which in some stories they also pass) is a divinatory tooth, allowing them to cut alphabetic twigs from the grove. An extraordinary detail! Words that grow on trees. Letters, language, words hidden in wood, basic to the wood itself, matter's own words, words that matter – the words in nature and the nature in words. So, indeed, this eye that can read trees is something to get hold of. It's like the origin of mythical vision and speech, cut from nature itself.

Perseus gets the eye by lying in wait, staying very still, so still as to be invisible (he was wearing the cap of Hades). Here the image of stopping is to wait quietly, until one is not, until even one's form and very self lapse nonexistent, invisible. An utter stillness, as T. S. Eliot says: "All in the waiting" – a kind of perfect attentiveness.

Then at a certain moment, between the movement of events out there, between the passing of the eye, one has it. For a moment one has the vision of the Graiae: that dark/light, old/young, ugly/beautiful, the rock as rose/rose as rock, animate/inanimate. For a moment one has captured a perception that opens the way to the Medusa's cave.

In the next image Perseus passes "boarlike into the cave." Now this is a very strange image. How is it that Perseus becomes like a boar? More specifically, how is it that this single eye of the Graiae, terrible beautiful stasis, makes the way become boarlike – fleshy, rutting, hurtling into the cave? From quiet stasis and a moment of perception we get now compulsion, a one-eyed thrust into darkness.

Surely the single eye is unpsychological, cycloptic. There's no "second sight" to "balance" vision, to give perspective, distance, reflection. With a single eye one is the eye – narrow, urgent, and animal-like. So it seems, but the pig leads into the Underworld, which is another word for the Medusa's cave. Also we remember Eubuleus's pigs who plunged through the Earth to the Underworld at the same moment as Persephone. So one way of entering this insubstantial realm of Underworld is with all the concrete, fleshy drive of a charging boar. One enters through immediacy.

Evidently, the Graiae's eye and divinatory tooth – that single straight perception – release an animal energy, an instinctual certainty where acting and perceiving are one thrust, like a boar. But it is a dark, Underworld perception, a psychic surety, a thrust not into world, but into darkness.

In the Medusa's Underworld you can't look at things straight on. If you look at the Medusa, if you let your eyes perceive her, you turn to stone. There are only two things you can do. One, the most well-known, is to regard her indirectly, look at her as a reflection by means of Athena's shield. Now this way of looking is guarded and self-protective, Athena as defense.

We in archetypal psychology have put this defense to good use. We have insisted upon reflection. It is crucial, we say, not to take things – events, dreams, emotions, urges – straight on literally but to reflect them as images. But there are many modes of reflection, none of which is always appropriate. For example, should I reflect with two eyes using Athena's shield while moving like a one-eyed boar, I would be undoing the very image I am in – an image whose instinctual power depends upon a one-eyed thrust, a movement straight into the thing, a master stroke. To hold up Athena's shield of reflection at a time like that would divide me from the pig who is my carrier and whose instinctual consciousness is the way.

Another problem with using Athena's shield to approach the Gorgon is that Athena doesn't like Gorgons. She gives them place because she's politic and wise, but that doesn't mean she likes them. In fact, there are tales that it was she who made the Medusa ugly in the first place. According to one story, the Medusa was a pretty girl who happened to be on the wrong side in a battle, and so Athena cursed her. According to another, the Medusa rivaled Athena's beauty and so was cursed. In yet another the Medusa as a horse made love with Poseidon in Athena's temple and for this sacrilege was cursed.

Athena's origin is also radically different from that of the Earth deities; she's a father's daughter who came out of a head, not a womb or the Earth. Altogether she has wonderful virtues and powers – a clear-eyed sense of balance, persuasion, politic inclusiveness – and I wouldn't wish to offend her. Still, I'd like to move another way: there's a second story, a variation of the myth in which Perseus uses no shield but averts his face and, letting fortune guide his hand, feels for the head of the Medusa.

Feeling – you *feel* the Medusa. You touch, sense her quality as mistress (her name means "the mistress"). Rather than reflection through distance, the image here is intimate, reflective sensitivity, Athena in the touch – that other Athena, Athena of the crafts, Athena in the hand.

But it's not easy, for the Medusa has long been regarded as an image of horror. The Greeks saw her as terrifying. As we approach the heroic, we experience her as a stopping, static threat. Progress dreads stasis, regards it even as an evil. Movement, development, activity appear all for the good, whereas to be stopped is to be afflicted. As of course we all are, and so we dread the Medusa's nature, push it away, dare not touch.

Now Perseus is warned against looking directly at the Medusa, and we learn in the tale of his wily way of indirection. But let us stop and focus on her: Why doesn't she want to be looked at directly? Could it be that to look at creates a distance that offends her, makes her an object, whereas I become removed, a spectator? To view her as an object creates this chasm between us, her and me, separating me from the depths of my nature. As she becomes objectified, I become "unnatural" or denatured – that heroic posture we have come to call ego consciousness.

We all know what happens to spectators in myths: Psyche looks into that box and falls down dead, Orpheus loses his bride, Actaeon gets torn to pieces, Pentheus ends up a basket case in his mad mother's lap. And when I look at the mysteries of my nature, objectify them, perceive them as though they were things, concepts – my sexuality, my body, my appetites, my feelings – the moment they become "things" to be worked on, adjusted, fixed, explained, I've lost them. That's the Medusa's revenge on those who approach her directly. Wham! My sexuality *becomes* a thing, my feelings conceptual, literal – "I'm feeling aggression. I'm getting anxious." My natural appetites and pains become objectified so that I must take care of myself with objects – pills, vitamins, minerals, quantitative exercises, set rules – my nature becomes numbered and inanimate. That is how the Medusa stops us dead. No wonder the Perseus myth is so recurrently valid. He is indeed the culture hero who saves us from this petrified objectivity.

The Medusa can get any of us when we see nature (her nature, my nature) as an objective fact detached from, out of touch with, the inner sensate touch of life. But Perseus finds a way, in the version of the tale I prefer, through touch. By touching the Medusa's body he traces its stasis, the outlines of its fixity, without distancing himself from it. He acknowledges that nature is as she is, simply there, but he keeps his hands on her and knows her body through his fingertips. He is intimate, concrete, near, abandoning the eye's direct perception of looking at, which makes for distance.

Through touch Perseus gets the Medusa's head, her very essence, and straps it to his back, backs himself with her immobility, her eternal deathlike vision. Thus backed, he is protected from the Gorgons. He's protected because he is backed by a vision that sees the immobility, the stasis, the rock in all things. If one can experience the stasis, can back oneself with that vision, then movement is possible, because movement is her nature too, is part of her very image – her eternally writhing hair.

Entering the Medusa's cave is like going into the blocked place, the frozen mood, the complex in which nothing moves, the incestuous bind, and then feeling it, feeling it in detail in one's fingers, touching; and in touching, discriminating, getting its head, its essence. Thus backed, movement is there and things animate.

Now Pegasus emerges from the headless body of Medusa: the great winged horse soars out. We have come to our final image – an image of most powerful animation. We mentioned earlier how the Medusa was once herself a horse and in that horse form made love with Poseidon in Athena's temple, for which transgression Athena turned Medusa ugly. Pegasus is the offspring of that temple copulation, so evidently not only was Medusa cursed with ugliness but also Pegasus was caught, imprisoned inside her, locked within her like spirit trapped in matter.

In this case, the spirit is an animal, a horse, that energetic beast of civilization, horse power. Could it be that our Athena consciousness, with all its bridling of animals (she invented the bridle), has lost touch with the animal itself? (Her animal, the owl, is seer par excellence, the very organ – eyes – not fit for the Medusa problem.)

In Athena's cursing the Medusa for her beastly sexuality, horselike in the temple, could it be that lower material things, the oldest goddesses (sow, phallic mother, Graiai, the Medusa) – those basest, most basic creatures of the mythic, those who hold and are the secret of stasis and animation – have been cursed, lost, frozen to our perception?

Wings: there are wings on Pegasus. He is wings with the body of a horse. Within the immovable stoniness of Medusa, moving in her depths, we find the power of air, a magnificent horse that carries one with the speed of thought. Here is mind and imagination that is also sinew, flank, muscle, and mane. A phallic stallion, a foaling mare rearing into the air. There are wings here beyond the bees and butterflies and little cherubic angels – wings that stomp and snort, that buck and gallop. So within nature's depths, its matter, we find a body of air; within stasis we find movement; in that awe-full image of stopping there is a rush of wings, an animal power in the insubstantial air.

SHADOW

X

On Reduction

"It was a great mistake on Freud's part to turn his back on philosophy." [96]
So charges C. G. Jung and in so doing sets for himself "the bittersweet
drink of philosophical criticism" [97] as perpetual test, indispensable for
the making of psychology. By remaining critical, Jung never stopped
making psychology, but we have – insofar as we content ourselves with
the piling-up of amplification, the fitting of more and more cases into
our selfsame puzzle, the reiterations turned clockwork, without at the
same time or occasionally or at least making room for the bittersweet-
ness of criticism. It is curious that Jung uses the word "philosophy" for
this activity. Could he not as easily have said "psychology" (that is to
say, a psychologizing of one's psychology), a self-reflection, or awareness? – words we are all familiar with and find fitting to our field. Most
probably he did not use them for that very reason. He needed a word
outside and beneath our conceptual ken. Jung continues:

> ... philosophical criticism has helped me to see that every psy-
> chology – my own included – has the character of a subjective
> confession ... I know well enough that every word I utter car-
> ries with it something of myself – of my special and unique
> self with its particular history and its own particular world.

---

96 C.G. Jung, *Freud & Psychoanalysis*, Collected Works, trans. R. F. C. Hull,
vol. 4 (Princeton Univ. Press, 1961), par. 774.
97 Ibid.

> Even when I deal with empirical data I am necessarily speaking about myself.[98]

It is perhaps here, where the question arises of recognizing that every psychology that is the work of one man is subjectively colored, that the line between Freud and myself is most sharply drawn.

A further difference seems to me to consist in this, that I try to free myself from all unconscious and therefore uncriticized assumptions about the world in general. I say "I try," for who can be sure that he has freed himself from all of his unconscious assumptions?[99]

From the above we can now gather that what Jung means by "philosophy" in this particular context is not necessarily its rational or logical characteristics, but, rather, a basic questioning and, most importantly, a questioning not circuitously consumed by the very constructs it proposes to examine. And it is this psychologizing of one's psychology (for I think we can now call it that) which he declares to be the major difference between himself and Freud! It is with this critical spirit of Jung's that we turn to the idea of reduction.

*

The term is one we use loosely to refer to "what Freud did," that distinctly factual, simplistic, causal tracing backward that traps the personality in infantile events and prevents movement forward and into spirit. Reduction tends to stand for a familiar conglomeration of causal with factual with concrete (material), a lessening of number (from many considerations to fewer), a movement in time (back) and direction (lower) and away from spirit (evidently its opposite).

The reductive process sounds distinctly sinister, without hope, and rather un-Jungian. And yet Jung himself assumes its need.[100] What is this

---

98 Ibid.
99 Ibid., par. 775–76.
100 On reduction: as caustic tool, see *Two Essays in Analytical Psychology*, Collected Works, trans. R. F. C. Hull, vol. 7 (Princeton Univ. Press, 1967), par. 65f.; for resolving transference, *Practice of Psychotherapy*, Collected Works, trans. R. F. C. Hull, vol. 16 (Princeton Univ. Press, 1966), par.

apparent contradiction? To take the contradiction at face value would be to become what we consider Freudian in regard to the "Freudian aspects" of a case (and in the very worst sense, since by employing the Freudian method piecemeal as Jungians, we lack the blessings of that orthodoxy) and then to become Jungian when we wish to deal with spirit, making of Jungian psychology a meager discipline, valuable only after the Freudian reduction is over, when meaning is important and inflation no consideration. But inflation is always a consideration as is meaning. Spirit means nothing when disconnected from its home in psyche, and psyche nothing when severed from its roots in *materia*. If we are not to be Freudians in regard to all the areas that Jung says need reductive approach, what we need is a Jungian model of reduction. But in order to approach that we must first do some disentangling.

Reduction vs. Concretism

One aspect of the conglomerate we consider reduction has to do with the concrete. Reduction may move us toward the perceptible, "things," lumps of life seen as external facts and events. If we secretly feel that the answer to our and our patients' troubles lies in the discovery of a hidden fact about which our lives revolve, then the goal of our reduction is the concrete. But if, on the other hand, our hunch is that the trouble is of a different order and not necessarily buried in a fact, then we are on another track and oddly enough the same track Freud was on when he discovered seductions to be psychic rather than actual events. Freud was humiliated when it became evident that the seductions reported to him by his patients, and which he had made much of, certainly could

---

286, and CW 7, par. 96; for severe neuroses, CW 16, par. 24; when meaning is conscious, and difficulty, unconscious, CW 7, par. 68; to phylogenetic basis and elementary processes, CW 6 (above, n.49), par. 852, and CW 16, par. 282; to reality, CW 6, par. 427, CW 7, par. 88, and CW 8 (above, n.51), par. 46; to the primitive or natural, CW 8, par. 93–95, 109, and CW 4 (above, n.95), par. 679; to "simple" instincts, CW 16, par. 40; for youth, CW 7, par. 88; as Shadow realization, CW 16, par. 146; as dream, CW 8, par. 496–98; as dream antecedents, CW 8, par. 452; as the "objective" level of dream, CW 7, par. 128.

not have been the decisive cause of their neuroses and may never have even happened. After the first wave of his defeat had subsided, however, he was able to confide:

> Tell it not in Gath, publish it not in the streets of Askalon, in the land of the Philistines, but between you and me I have the feeling of a victory rather than of a defeat. [101]

Not only was Freud's realization a significant victory for the future of psychology, but also the metaphor into which he put this realization is more than notable. Whereas the Philistines would rejoice at his defeat, they would revenge a victory, so best they not be told. For victory it was – over the Philistines. By allusion Freud seemed to have recognized that concrete event could be as much an enemy to psychological insight as the common sense of the Philistine was antipathetic to the emergence of spirit. Psychology and fact, and thereby spirit and Philistine, had at this moment of Freud's realization become separate. But we may draw something even more significant from Freud's discovery: the Philistine as a psychological entity, an archetypal mode of perception, what philosophers have referred to as the "common sense man" or the "plain man." This archetypal mode would justify things in terms of their being "only natural," nothing-but, bread-and-butter, down-to-earth, factual, practical. The perceptible, the material, would be for this viewpoint the "real facts" of life.

Both before and in many ways after this psychological realization of 1897, Freud proceeded Philistine intact, unaware of its workings. It was "only natural" that he take at face value his patients' reports. In this case, it wasn't until events no longer made sense to the Philistine himself – the facts just didn't make sense – that Freud was forced to admit a defeat that seemed at the time his own defeat (his hopes of success and

---

101 E. Jones, *Sigmund Freud: Life and Work* (London: Hogarth Press, 1953), vol. I, 294. Cf. 2 Samuel 1.19ff.: *Your glory, O Israel, lies slain / upon your high places! How the mighty have fallen! /Tell it not in Gath, /publish it not in the streets of Ashkelon; /or the daughters of the Philistines will rejoice, /the daughters of the uncircumcised will exult.*

wealth were "dashed to the ground" [102]) and to move on toward his real success: the founding of depth psychology.

What Freud alluded to as Philistine consciousness has generally been treated developmentally. Mankind in the course of time has developed from this primitive concrete thinking toward more independent, abstract thinking. But if, as we have suggested, the Philistine is also an archetype, then we must expect its continual reappearance. Freud did not get rid of it. For Jung, Freud even became it.

Jung's objections to Freud's mechanistic reductivism attest to Jung's own struggle with the Philistine, albeit now through the work of Freud. The struggle was fitting, because the common sense to which the Philistine reduces all events is necessarily an enemy to emerging psychological spirit – Freud's, Jung's, whomever's. But certainly we cannot dispense with the concrete mode. It is after all a necessary function upon which we depend for basic orientation and likewise for all situations in which action is more important than mind, doing more important than reflecting, object more important than image, practice more important than theory, the perceptible more important than the thinkable. But if this concretistic mode is archetypal, so, too, are the battles in which it is involved. Do we learn by doing, or is our doing a consequence of having first conceived? Do we theorize from the observable or observe on the basis of our theory? Which comes first is a question of philosophic and archetypal preference. Which archetypal mode is really most basic, most "real"? And of course we each end up with our particular mixtures, such as Jung's empiricism-cum-Platonism or Freud's materialism-cum-mythologism. Somehow psychology realizes that logical consistency would make for fallacious theory.

So our problem is not consistency, but, rather, a psychological awareness of which mode we are using where. In the case of the concrete, this awareness is extremely difficult, because at the moment of realizing that we are using it, that we are now concrete, we are already partly out, partly metaphorical, relativizing our standpoint. The telltale mark of concrete procedures is one's total ignorance of having

---

102 Jones, *Sigmund Freud* (above, n.100), 293.

used them: one merely *is*, things merely *are*. To be concretistic one must be identical with the procedure one is using, the viewpoint one is in. Furthermore, like any archetypal problem or perspective, when the concrete mode becomes entangled with other equally valid procedures, it works to their detriment. But the concretistic mode is especially damaging to psychology,especially dangerous to spirit, because it is by nature anti-psychic and anti-spirit. For Freud it was a sturdy Goliath wanting no nonsense. But in whatever form it appears, the point is that it be located and grappled with – ceaselessly, it would seem, if one's business is depth psychology.

Jung, too, evokes the Philistine when referring to "Jesus' challenge to Nicodemus":

> Do not think carnally, or you will be flesh, but think symbolically, and then you will be spirit… for Nicodemus would remain stuck in banalities if he did not succeed in raising himself above his concretism. Had he been a mere Philistine, he would certainly have taken offence at the irrationality and unreality of this advice and understood it literally, only to reject it in the end as impossible and imcomprehensible… The empirical truth never frees a man from his bondage to the senses… The symbolical truth… canalizes it into a spiritual form. [103]

For spirit, in particular, the danger of the concretistic is its inertia, its only-too-natural gravitational pull downward into matter. It is understandable that much of religious tradition came to view matter as black and formless, the opposite of light (Delilah is popularly taken to be a Philistine); the flesh as sinful; the bull as requiring defeat; Egypt requiring exodus, and so on. The Philistine played a major role indeed in the history of the Church – so major that in the continuous attempts to expurgate him, much of the concrete was thrown into his company as well. The animal, the body, the dark, the sensual, the feminine lost psychic significance. No distinction had been made between the merely concrete and the concretistic attitude, better called literalism.

---

103 C.G. Jung, *Symbols of Transformation*, Collected Works, trans. R. F. C. Hull, vol. 5 (Princeton Univ. Press, 1967), par. 335.

Literalism

Because our aim is psyche – and psyche has as much to do with matter as with spirit – we can have no quarrel with the concrete as such. Body, objects, the sensible-perceptible, facts, images are all the prima materia upon which, and even within which, the psyche operates. Rather, we quarrel with the literalism that would take these objects only at face value, robbing them of metaphorical value, i.e., soul significance.

When in his own land – the land of the concrete, nature, things as they are – the Philistine has an archetypal survival value. But when he is confronted with the Hebrews (read religious or psychological spirit), whose opus is against that nature, the Philistine becomes then the enemy. He applies his concrete attitudes where they do not belong: this makes for literalism.

An unfortunate result is that this literalism then blocks the way to the concrete. When approaching the concrete, we meet instead the literal. Body, for example, then becomes only body, and we miss its metaphorical nature. The true sin of the flesh lies in its literal nothing-but interpretation, not in the flesh itself. Thus by shunning the sin, as the spiritual instinct necessarily does, we tend to miss the body as well. So our continuous need to redeem body from the literalism with which it is perceived, to free matter from a false spirit, which becomes reversed into freeing spirit from matter. Because the Philistine keeps literalizing matter, we are driven to fight him there, in matter, to redeem matter, whereas the sin is the literalism in which he has encased it. Thus it is even difficult to discover the appropriate matter with which to begin, difficult to return to nature, body, or anything concrete, without returning to the literalistic attitude as well.

An image at the end of Plato's *Symposium* might make this point clearer. We know that Socrates is a lover, a drinker, and a soldier. He can enjoy and endure the concrete. Moreover, in the passage we have in mind, Alcibiades compares Socrates to the wooden statue of a Silenus, that most concrete satyr. Yet when the little doors to this figure are opened, the images of the gods are revealed within. [104] The literalistic

---

104 *Symposium* 215bff.

attitude would see the satyr and stop there, missing the gods within. But once we have seen through the literal representation, the concrete body is itself a metaphor.

Curiously enough, when the concrete is denied, as in the case of the spiritual denial of body, images, or the senses, a concretism (or literalism) appears in its place within the spirit itself. Not only do the body, the images, or the senses, which are innocent enough and useful enough as modes of the concrete, become loaded with the literalistic weight of anti-spirit and anti-psyche, but also the concrete mode is displaced upward, creating literalisms of the spirit. This is the Philistines' revenge. The concrete that was defeated comes back to carry the day as literalisms. These appear as reified thinking, hypostasized ideas and metaphysical substances, and religion's investment in the letter of its dogma.

Hence Jung's lifelong battle to separate his ideas from Plato's hypostasized forms as well as from the substantials of the metaphysicians. Jung's aim was to keep the psyche free both from the left, Freud's literalization of sexuality, and from the right, the hypostasization of the metaphysicians. His course was to be that most subtle way of the metaphor, as yet uncharted by psychology.

In the spirit of this "as-if," Jung insisted that his archetypes be viewed as psychic "possibilities," an insistence significant in light of Freud's reified archaic "memories." But Jung's deliteralization that is most often referred to appears in his treatment of the Oedipal question. For Jung, sexuality, apart from its concrete natural function, was psychologically meaningful in its symbolic aspect. Metaphorically incest had to do with "union with one's own being... simply the union of like with like, which is the next stage in the development of the primitive idea of self-fertilization."[105] This did not mean, of course, that he was advocating incest: rather, that he was distinguishing its metaphorical from its literal interpretation. On the question of the incest taboo, Jung responded with an anthropological argument, a concrete-literal answer, thereby putting the Philistine in his archetypal and appropriate place, the realm of practical considerations.[106]

---

105 CW 16 (above, n.99), par. 419.
106 CW 5 (above, n.102), par. 217.

What Freud implied by Philistinism, Jung elaborated in terms of primitive thinking. "Primitive thinking and feeling are entirely concretistic; they are always related to sensation. The thought of the primitive has no detached independence but clings to material phenomena." [107] In primitive functioning, symbols are not distinct from object awareness. Symbols are literalized. What for the "primitive" *is* becomes for us in our sophisticated awareness *as-if.* The "primitive" appears in the natural. So when we sense our 'natural' viewpoint emerging, our "it's-only-natural" explanations, we must look as well to the underlying primitive *is*, the hidden literalism to which it is bound.

The innocent babe in the woods, the nymphic maidens, the nature spirits – trolls, elves, dwarfs, dactyls – bring us not only sparks of natural consciousness, but also hidden literal qualities. They carry not only the release of a complex but somewhere else its fixation. The magic of the wood spirit has to do with the magic in primitive thinking, that literalistic attitude that binds psyche to physical signs and events. When I dream of the tricky little dwarf, I find in waking life new perceptions, quick insights, intuitive sparks.

The world takes on a sense of magic and fairy-tale adventure. I jump from task to task as if enchanted, and the smallest events assume psychic significance; I see synchronicities and meanings everywhere. But psyche and concrete nature have merged into a narcissistic state, so that not only am I the world but the world is I, and psyche itself takes on a form as literal as the concrete objects to which it is attached. The bird that passed by, the letter in my mail box, the pot that boiled over are no longer only concrete facts but now have become pregnant with pseudo-psyche. Psyche has become magically bound to the literal events in which it has been discovered. It is as though the possibilities given by the nature spirits with one hand, the possibilities of psyche, are taken back with the other, the demand to be taken literally. The very moment we discover psyche, where before there were only concrete events, we again lose psyche to those same events, now taken literally.

---

107 CW 6 (above, n.49), par. 697.

The voice in us that says, "but that is the way it is!" Jung would place with the primitive, first level of the psyche, thereby emphasizing its initial self-protective purpose. Because of this voice we would know when to run, whom to avoid, that there is an out-there to be reckoned with. The difficulty, however, is like that with the Philistine, the image we have used for Jung's primitive. What then takes more subtle, more metaphorical handling is taken up likewise by this literal voice. When this voice is in its most pathological form, we hear real voices, see real visions, take our fantasies and projections as "true." As an example of this, Jung mentions the primitive who dreamt that he was burned alive and who, in order apotropaically to avert this misfortune, put his feet in the fire and was badly burned. [108]

This inability to take the dream other than literally, and likewise other than concretely to act out an attempt at its aversion, shows stunningly how literalism can make for a circularity, landing one in exactly the situation one had sought, by means of literalism, to avoid. This happens each time we take the danger in a dream as a literal warning and act to avert it. As with the primitive, such literalism leads to a chain of undoing. When I avoid the person who constellates the worst in me, what he represents becomes all the more literally constellated in my psyche. I reinforce the literal quality of this psychic constellation (and any constellation has its Philistine face), making greater the possibility of my literally acting it out and then undoing it with an opposite and even more literal factor in order to keep the initial threat in abeyance. Then this undoing has to be undone too. So I proceed through a chain of literalisms misusing dreams as guides for my actions.

Since, as we have said, any psychic constellation has its literal aspect and can be taken literally, the problem in therapy becomes one of recognition and discrimination of the literal archetype. But the task is not easy, primarily because the plain man literalist also has his say about what psychology is and what it means to be psychological. Nevertheless, let us consider an example: the choice problem, the problem that "calls for a decision." Since the call for a decision already

---

108 CW 8 (above, n.51), par. 94.

casts the situation into literal terms – should I or shouldn't I – the natural course would be to meet the problem within the area it has set for itself. Then we would discuss it with our analysts or, even better, with ourselves, swapping literalisms between parts of the psyche, giving to ourselves opinions drawn on past experience and practical counseling – all of which would meet the Philistine's view of what is psychological. Especially, this self-counseling would have reference to the facts: finances, schedules, advantages and disadvantages – my dinner last night, my mother's visit, my economic situation.

Another alternative would be to refuse the decision altogether, to hold that psyche has nothing to do whatsoever with the literal decisions of life. This is perhaps what psychoanalysis implies by its rule that no major alterations in the life situation be undertaken during the course of the analysis. A marriage, a divorce, a change in jobs would be at that time merely an acting out.

Whereas the first of these ways of meeting the problem of decision identifies life as psyche so that working on life and solving its problems hold the illusion of working on psyche, the second position places life as opposed to psyche, maintaining that they have nothing directly to do with each other. Both of these positions make life literal, and both deny the metaphorical, thereby disregarding Jung's statement that "every interpretation necessarily remains an 'as-if.'"

There is yet a third alternative. This would be to refuse the practical discussion of the problem until we have had the right dream and then to connect the dream with the problem. Here we feel we are being truly psychological, connecting psyche and life. But let us see by an example how this might work:

Say I am an American in Europe trying, once again, to decide whether or not to go back to America. Should I have had a "positive dream" of an American Indian, that would portend going. But just here the literalist has his victory, for he has made of the dream an oracle. Like a primitive he has magically confused metaphor with the literal. And, more importantly, he has insisted that the dream, by either its confirmation or its denial, must correspond with a literal reality. The dream must serve the problem; the metaphorical must provide an answer to the literal.

The psyche has been forced into serving the concerns of the Philistine. This occurs even when we least notice it. When, for example, I say I cannot continue with this plan, work, relationship because my dreams won't let me, I feel I am sacrificing the outer for the sake of the inner. I feel that the outer is serving the inner. But still I am reading the inner as a confirmation, warning, or denial of the outer. And the real loss is not the plan, work, relationship – but the psyche.

The literalist not only has taken my quandary – should I or shouldn't I – at face value but also has robbed my psyche of its dignity. He has not respected psyche as a function every bit as valid in its own right as is the ego with its decisions. To give the psyche its due would be to recognize the literalism (decision problem) as the reflection of a fantasy, a way in which the fantasy is expressing itself. Because the fantasy has been taken up by the literalist, I now want to know what to *do*, practically speaking. I think that is my problem, as the literalist always thinks his concerns are the problem. Decision-making itself benefits the literalist, confirms him, and makes him stronger. Neglected are the psychological values in the metaphors "America," "home," "going back" (both in the sense of regression and in the sense of return), as well perhaps as the counterpole of "exile," "alien," "foreign," "outside the fold" (and all the pathology inherent in these), to say nothing of "crossing the great water"!

The point would be to find the metaphorical background, the context from which the literalism emerged, actually to see the literalism psychologically – and by so deliteralizing, to return it to psyche. Like Perseus, we must see this Gorgon through a mirror, through the reflection of metaphor, else we become the Gorgon ourselves, meeting literal with literal and thereby neglecting the reflective indirection of the psychological.

After this analytic hour with himself, the literalist feels, of course, vaguely dissatisfied. He had expected to come out with a clear list of reasons for-and-against or to turn the Indian of the dream into a magical "coincidence," which would thereby solve the problem. Yet in some way, too, this plain man has been relieved, his ferric nature softened and made more yielding; the weight of ego identification with which he has been burdened has been shifted to wider and more fertile, metaphorically more substantial ground.

Part of the great difficulty we have with the literalist is that he operates relatively and therefore cannot easily be pinned down. He does not always say the same thing or have the same viewpoint. He appears anyway less in literal definitions than in a literalistic attitude that can shift from one aspect of the psyche to another. We see this in our interpretations of the dream ego.

Given a certain sophistication, probably the most concrete mode a dream interpreter could fall into would be to take the dream ego as identical with the most literal aspect of the waking ego: dream ego = I. (I should not go off this weekend because I have just dreamed I was in a car accident.) A second level of interpretation would be to distinguish the waking "I" from the dream ego. (In this dream my ego is doing such and such – not I, but my ego.) In this case, the "I" that works on the dream is at least given a point of reflection over and above that of the dream ego. A further level of deliteralization then would take this particular dream reflection as an attitude, one of the many guises, of the ego. (My ego is here behaving in its role of spoiled child, kind parent, successful general, or whatever.) Yet further would be to see that this particular guise is the result of the interplay of the dream scene, dependent upon it, and that the reality of the dream is only in terms of its participants. When my ego is doing this and this, then the dream setting is particularly such and the participants constellated in a certain manner. The point here is to realize the context within the dream itself, the particularity spun out of the relationships among all the parts. To draw any behavioral precepts or "shoulds" out of the dream constellation would be again to take it literally and out of its own metaphorical context, neglecting the real and psychological task: to lay out and analyze the constellation, to sharpen and fill out the metaphor that the psyche has presented, and to resist the cheapening predictions, the temptations of the Philistine, his practical advice.

Toward a Psychological Reduction

We may return once again to the question of reduction. If the process of reduction must be identical with the literalism we have been discussing, as Jung supposed when speaking of Freud's reduction, then certainly, since our business is psychology and soul-making, such reduction would lead us very far astray. Yet again we must ask ourselves why Jung – who never ceased to stress the "as-if," who championed metaphor against so many Philistines, who never spoke in terms of nothing-but, by which he defined reduction – nevertheless did speak of the need for a reductive process. My suspicion is that Jung intuited something very much deeper about the essential nature of this process than was apparent in its practice. Jung was not contradicting himself when he both stressed its need and yet denied its methods. Was he perhaps sensing another kind of reduction, one devoid of the literal and in keeping with his own psychology?

His later alchemical work certainly returns Jung to reduction. There we delve into what had been the seeds of his earlier intuition. By that time Jung no longer mentions the term reduction, with its Freudian associations, as a tool of analysis. Perhaps Jung's own sort of reduction had already made its way into his thought, via the more highly differentiated concepts within alchemy. One must note the reductive significance of processes such as *mortificatio, putrefactio, separatio, calcinatio, coagulatio*. Such reductions have little to do with literalism, though their basic metaphors involve concrete substances. In one notable passage, Jung even uses the term reduction as synonymous with the psychological idea of synthesis. "The aim of the tetrasomia is the reduction (or synthesis) of a quaternio of opposites to unity." [109]

As reduction in the Freudian sense would connote a return to beginnings, a causal tracing back in time to childhood, the primal scene, the Oedipal complex, the basic traumas and libidinal fixations, so alchemy would move toward beginnings – the *radix* elements or the *prima materia*,

---

109 C.G. Jung, *Alchemical Studies*, Collected Works, trans. R. F. C. Hull Princeton Univ. Press, 1968), vol. 13, par. 358.

in any of its many forms. A basic difference, however, does appear in the use of cause. Freud's use is more literal, more mechanical, more in the sense of *causa efficiens*. Psychoanalysis leads one back in time, through actual life history, and toward causes buried in the earliest years. Reduction is taken literally as reduction, leading back or leading again, in the sense that going through the same events again may free one from them. Alchemical reduction moves rather toward the *prima materia* at the core of the complex, which need not be seen as prior in time but as prior in ontology, status, or value. This unformed is never fully formed and always present. It is as it is always. As a core it is the basic matter of what's the matter, and it is always described by the alchemists in metaphorical terms, terms of outlandish perplexity so that one could not possibly confuse them with actual incidents of an actual life.

Because the entire alchemical process is based on the metaphors of the *prima materia*, the process, too, is metaphorical, even if here our literal man jumps again into the works to take "the process" literally. This time he attempts to make process a linear event in which each successive stage transforms the preceding and thereby most probably loses it. Because of the literalist's penchant for "process," "complex" gives us perhaps a better image, for its definition insists upon a nucleus, an archetypally (as-if, metaphorically) based, pathological core to which increasing numbers of associations adhere. Nothing is overcome or left behind, because the movement is not literally linear. Instead, projections are taken back, dissociations rejoined, all of which leaves one feeling much sicker than before. Whether one *is* sicker or not is another matter – a matter of great interest to the plain man in us all. We want to see progress and so strive to set up some criterion which answers this need. We pay actual money and sit actual hours with our analysts and, in keeping with this constellation, expect actual cure or actual betterment.

Yet this literalism, too, is sooner or later broken and replaced more metaphorically, for *we feel* sicker, our sense of sickness having become perhaps more subtly attuned. The health/sickness dichotomy has merged into a more highly differentiated sense of daily-life pathology. By deliteralizing diagnostic prototypes, we see their "as-if" relevance in our own lives – our "as-if" schizoid or paranoid mechanisms, our areas of psychopathy or hysterical responses. This is not, by any means, to devalue the real sicknesses as described by psychiatry, but, rather, to see them as prototypes, "reals" from which to make metaphor. If I have not acquired this sense of sickness, then either my analysis has not intended to touch the pathology (or archetypes) at all, or it has refused to proceed in that direction because of its literal ideas of reduction as something only negative, only destructive, only Freudian.

Reduction gives the sense of pathology and, at the same time, because it is deliteralized, makes pathology meaningful. Pathology becomes the touchstone of the psychological. The difference between me and my mental hospital prototype becomes qualitative rather than quantitative: she more literal in her psychic connection, I more metaphorical. But the root of the matter (our psychic matter) is similar. Should I, in the course of my analysis, remain still separate from my sickness, encapsulated and protected, then the benefits of my analysis, the changes in my awareness, the conscious insights should all be called into question and examined to see if they, too, are not just additional, albeit more complicated, more subtle (and therefore more insidious) defenses, my very individuation a defensive system. But certainly if my pathology seems to have disappeared, my analysis has failed. And the failure is due to a faulty view of reduction.

Reduction keeps us in touch with prime psychic matter. Because as Jungians we make much of building (synthetic approach), finality, process as progression, and the teleological implications of completion, wholeness, becoming conscious, transcendent function, we are ever in danger of losing a sense of the depths. If we give reduction away to the Freudians, we lose one of the ways of maintaining this depth. Without our own kind of reduction, even the opposites, which were meant by Jung as a means of deepening, a way of realizing the ambiguity and complexity of psychic life, become instead an ego defense, a way of balancing, and thus a way of keeping out of the depths.

The whole point of reduction is precisely that it goes too far, off the end of the balance, to the roots. Its aim is the radical moisture, the *radix ipsius*, [110] the "secret hidden in the roots," [111] the prime matter to which there is no opposite, no other principle, but which contains in its radicality its own internal opposition. To go down and back merely because it leads up and forward, to confront the negative with the positive (or vice versa), or to apply a bit of reduction as a therapeutic technique in order to "integrate some Shadow" is perhaps an artificiality, probably a simplicity, but assuredly a literalism. When the opposites are taken in this manner, the aspiring mathematician, wildly spinning formulas in his attic, is told to come down to earth and take up gardening, or to live among the peasants in the mountains and chop his own firewood. Had Einstein "balanced" his life by chopping firewood, the world most probably would have had no Einstein. He probably would have cut off his foot, thereby leaving the theory of relativity spinning footless in the heavens. But his theories had a foot, and they were grounded; within his eccentricity the opposites were at work and to the benefit of the world. [112] According to Jung, once a person

> ... has seen the Faustian problem, the escape into the "simple life" is closed for ever. There is of course nothing to stop him from taking a two-room cottage in the country, or from pottering about in a garden and eating raw turnips. But his soul laughs at the deception. Only what is really oneself has the power to heal. [113]

What is really oneself can only emerge out of one's nature but not out of a nature that has been recommended.

For when the balancing of the opposites is taken up by the literalist, it becomes a prescription a priori rather than a description a posteriori, thereby cutting off the possibility of an individual, or unique, develop-

---

110 C. G. Jung, *Psychology and Alchemy*, Collected Works, trans. R. F. C. Hull Princeton Univ. Press, 1968), vol. 12, par. 430.

111 CW 13 (above, n.108), par. 242f.

112 That Einstein was in some ways a "simple man" is beside the point in this context, for whatever simplicity he had – he wore no socks we know – his extremity remained intact. For us, that is the decisive factor.

113 CW 7 (above, n.99), par. 258.

ment before it begins. When Jung said that *les extremes se touchent*, he did not mean it as a literal device to be put into practical application, touching each thing with a bit of its opposite, especially since the opposite for each psychic content cannot be known in advance. It is the unconsciousness buried in the reduced state itself. Compensation and balancing by opposites – because they are in the hands of the literalist who has his ready-made high for every low (and low for every high), his literal inner for every outer, etc. – are to be eschewed until we are quite sure the Philistine and the daughters of the Philistine and their daughters' daughters have all been through a psychological analysis. Of all the haunts of the plain man (and he has many, as we have seen, such as process, primitivity, practicality, naturalness, life, magical synchronicity), none is more ruinous to the spirit of Jung's open-endedness than the neat little scales of compensation. The literalist wields the opposites in such a way as to make everyone more or less similar and like himself, a literalist and mediocre. The median and the statistical average are this same sort of balance in another form. This is not the uniqueness of self that Jung's work evokes.

Psychology has traditionally focused its study upon the extremes, the aberrant, the pathological. Reduction would mean a return to these. Psychology's tradition is in the area of reduction, the area of the radical and the extreme: the extremity of our misfortune, the trapped aspect of fate, the un-understandable. Jung speaks of the hopelessness, the resignation in the reduced. And indeed what one seems to find, or at least expects to find, through the process of reduction is expressed as negative: putrefaction, mortification, nigredo. Even the fire of reduction is negative "because it burns all things and reduces them to powder: quicksilver is vinegar," [114] the tincture a "fiery and gaseous poison." [115]

Here Mercurius himself has turned sour, and there is no compensatory sweetness.

Reduction's extreme is a concentrate of Shadow, that which would undermine our ego's positions, no matter how "balanced," "right," or

114 CW 13 (above, n.108), par. 103n.
115 Ibid., par. 358n.

reasonably attuned. Reduction, blacking in ego's shadows, tones gray ego's tightness. The alchemical idea of the gold in the dung would reverse rather to show the dung in the gold. Wherever there is gold – each goal attained, each piece of conscious realization – would be also where to look for the dung. The best smells worst. But to be never far from the dung heap is also psychic body. Whereas all gold looks alike, psychic body makes for discrimination. Each complex has its own smell to the nose of instinct, and thus gold-making would require the help of reductive discrimination.

The negative tone of reduction still needs to be explained. Of course, it belongs to the Shadow or personal unconscious, to which Jung said it applied. However, its unpleasantness, difficulty, and extremity refer to the *senex*. And so our theme is oppressed by the lead of Saturn. Owing to this archetype, reduction is inevitably seen leadenly, opaquely, as concrete, and as literal. Saturn forces reduction into the literalism of dirt, history, negativity, resignation, hopeless causality, depression. Even the primitivity of reductive thinking belongs to Saturn, who ruled at the beginning of time. Just as reduction prevents forward movement, Saturn swallowed his own children. But if we stop there, we have again reduced reduction to a nothing-but. For Saturn as well frees from the very literalisms he fosters. Saturn, the principle of abstraction, sees through to the ultimate realities. Perhaps this is what the journey through the planetary houses signifies, both beginning and ending with Saturn,[116] or the image of the white dove contained in the lead.[117]

A psychological reduction, and by this we imply one freed of all the literalisms to which reduction has been reduced – concretism, historicism, causalism, simplistic Freudianism, etc. – would be one of the operations of psychological work. It would go toward the extreme *radix*. It would be the way of arriving at the irreducible, the essential oil, the quintessence of one's nature, the indelible character traits that are concealed in the dross of one's case history.

116 CW 14 (above, n.47), par. 298–311.
117 CW 12 (above, n.109), par. 443.

Through these character traits, one is involved with the *daimones* of one's fate and with the *prima materia* in the daily entanglement with literal problems which, because they are *prima materia*, give the psyche the chance to move them from the literal to the metaphorical, thereby giving ground and body, relief to the literal itself. Reduction denies the free and easy flow of life. It makes for difficulties, constructs obstacles; it dams up and dampens down. Jung had in mind reduction as literal and thus its goal as natural. But when reduction is viewed as metaphorical, the end becomes *contra naturam* as well. Viewed metaphorically, *naturam* and *contra naturam* are one. Only the literal is solely *naturam*; and once world, nature, body, matter are seen as image, sensed as metaphor, they are in psyche transformed. Reduction by going into the concrete and the natural is the *via regia* of the *opus contra naturam*.

XI

The Training of Shadow and the Shadow of Training

I have always found the Shadow the most difficult of psychological experiences, even though it is supposed to be the first and so presumably the easiest. The Shadow is not difficult to understand conceptually. The idea is based on a model of opposites and Jung's notion of the one-sidedness of conscious functioning. What is easy to understand theoretically is practically and experientially more difficult. Part of the difficulty for me, I thought, had to do with my generation of the 1950s and 1960s in which conscious identifications were uncertain, since consciousness itself was uncertain. The generation Jung addressed appeared more solid, still a bit Victorian in its convictions. In that generation, there seemed a clear distinction between what the ego embraced and the Shadow undid. There was a light and a darkness of the light. There really were Dr. Jekylls and Mr. Hydes.

In my generation, we were "on the road" with Kerouac, wailing with Elvis, Fats Domino, Little Richard; we also embraced the virtues of science (there was a space race, and LSD was a chemical compound); we were idealistic (we marched for racial integration and burnt draft cards).

Now all of this confused emotionality (beatnik, scientific, idealistic) makes of the Shadow a complicated entity. First, there is not a Shadow, but many (as there is not one conscious standpoint, but many – all equally serious, depending upon the mood and the moment). Structures of awareness shift. What is relatively conscious at one moment is not at the next. As the source of light shifts, as position or situation changes (as a different light is cast on things), so the Shadow wanders.

I felt better about this shifting character of my Shadow when I came across a passage in Jung. In "On the Nature of the Psyche," Jung notes that "sliding consciousness," as he calls it, "is thoroughly characteristic of modern man." So it is not unusual after all. Jung goes on to explain why he prefers the word "shadow" to more scientific conceptualizations, even "the inferior part of the personality." The problem, he says, with these "scientific-looking Graeco-Latin neologism[s]" is that the content becomes fixed, so that one loses the suffering and passion that implicate the whole person. He prefers the word "shadow" because it is a poetic term, implying plasticity and an aesthetic, linguistic heritage. [118]

So the Shadow is connected with culture. It is not a term from scientific psychology or from moral theology; rather, it is an imagistic idea. The word itself has shadowy connotations, being inexact, nonstatic, varying over time and in different situations.

In keeping with Jung's poetic description of the Shadow, one might imagine the best training for Shadow awareness to be a poetic or aesthetic training. Now I do not mean necessarily poetry or painting. Nor do I mean literally that a candidate for training must have an academic background in the arts. Though I think that might be a good idea, at the moment at least I am referring to the arts as a metaphorical backdrop against which we might view our work with Shadow.

As a poetic (rather than a scientific) idea, the Shadow becomes difficult to define in general, as in the arts general laws seldom hold true. When one says a good poem is this and not that, one is in trouble, since in another poem, in another situation, the same criteria may not apply. Rather, what is required is a sharp eye to situation – the shape of the work, the behavior, the action, the feeling within a particular context.

What are the implications once we have assumed this aesthetic metaphor as background to our work? The first is that we, as craftsmen or artists of the psyche, begin with distinct, particular perceptions rather than with generalities into which particulars must then fit. In other words, in training for Shadow awareness we encourage the aesthetic

118 C. G. Jung, "On the Nature of the Psyche," CW 8 (above, n. 51), par. 409.

perception of particulars in lieu of global thinking, thinking in large general categories about the Shadow.

To the aesthetic eye, conceptual thinking obscures – or even loses – the Shadow. For example, even though it is theoretically, conceptually correct to regard the Shadow as the inferior part of the personality or as closer to the animal and the instinctual, in a particular situation that is often not the case – at least on an apparent level. As Jung frequently noted, the Shadow may be a superior part of the personality, a hidden talent, a figure more moral than the ego. Also, it need not be animal and instinctual; it may as well be disembodied, airy, rigid, anorexic.

Another way in which one may generalize Shadow, and thus aesthetically miss it, is by thinking of Shadow as only a moral problem. When looking for good and evil, black and white, one misses the colors and shades. In painting, for example, shadows are actually greens, purples, browns, deeper tones of the same color – not usually blacks. These shadows give form. Shadings make certain things stand out and others recede so that (as in a painting or building, poem or human face) depth, perspective, and substance become apparent.

There is a third way to miss the Shadow aesthetically. When traits, types, complexes, and syndromes are global general concepts, they lead us to miss the Shadow in particular. Let us say that my Shadow in general is extraverted feeling, laziness, pretentiousness. Whereas it's true all these traits are my Shadow, they do not really give me the *experience* of Shadow. Worse! They occlude the possibility of my experiencing Shadow. (Once I have conceptually' wrapped it up, I think I have already experienced it and so pay little further attention.)

Also what we tell others can block Shadow awareness. Recently I told an analysand that he was caught in the mother complex. Of course, this was an analytic *faux pas*, but I was weary that evening, and his insubstantial, clever talk irritated me. The whole of the next week he could only see his mother complex. In the following session, everything that happened to him he interpreted as a further instance of mother. He told of a scene with his wife, who accused him of not doing his share of the housework, not taking her out, not protecting her, not paying enough attention to her. He had concurred with all this because he "knew" that he had a mother complex, and so the discussion had stopped.

Of course, his giving in to the accusation, thus halting the discussion, *was* his mother complex! Armed with this general idea about himself (unfortunately given him by me), he used the generality to keep from perceiving or feeling anything sharp and detailed about himself, any particular value or Shadow shape.

The Shadow must threaten awareness, and nothing *in general* is really threatening. Only the specific and the unexpected hit us hard. The specific is intimate (close, small, near), and the unexpected is simply the unconscious itself. So the Shadow comes in specific and unexpected moments – in the moment I am baring my soul and also manipulating for sympathy; or when I am feeling love and genuine warmth for my analysand – then realize it is *my* need, and that I am also binding the analysand to me; or when I predict a marriage is breaking up – and realize my prediction is playing a role in the disaster, scheming it along; or, in the realm of thought, when I'm speaking intellectually and suddenly realize I am lost in my own abstraction.

There seems a certain masochistic enjoyment in Shadow awareness. We must like this suffering, else why do it? Something in us must delight as our ground collapses. Maybe this painful enjoyment of losing certainty is an aesthetic pleasure too – like the enjoyment of a good play or novel that upsets, turns round the way we have viewed things and, through the tensions it creates, forces on us another vision.

So we come to tension. Shadow awareness proceeds through tension, and again we find that the more specific or close our focus on shades of difference, the more the tension. It is the pink that clashes with the red because they are so close. Blue does not clash with red so much as it compensates or balances it, preventing the intimate tension that makes for specific Shadow awareness.

As an example of these tensions: a woman I work with in analysis is wildly libidinous, irrational, and "liberated" in her night life; whereas in her day life, she is rational, considered, responsible. These red and blue opposites stand side by side, balancing each other in a way that does not move and makes psychic work difficult. Although the red and blue sides of her personality are large-scale opposites, they are not effective Shadows. They do not create tension, nor would they make an interesting painting. A psychologically working tension, a moving tension, would be between her softly pink sentimental notions of love and her red hot-tin-roof nights. Then her pink and red would be in tension.

This aesthetic emphasis on the particular is like Jung's insistence on the individual – the unique against which he posited the collective. Jung eschewed large systems and organizations; he keenly distrusted general strictures. As a good clinician, Jung was a craftsman, an aesthetician.

So far I have looked at the Shadow against an aesthetic backdrop in order to emphasize its multiplicity, specificity, and subtlety. Now I would like to move more directly into Jungian terminology – where the specific is called "the individual," the unique, and the general or broadly conceived becomes "the collective." Since relationship with the collective is a current issue in our training programs, I would like to go into Jung's notions of the collective in some detail.

Jung has three psychological nuances in his use of "the collective." Most negatively, the collective is the mass, the crowd, the mob – Hitler's Germany. In this idea of the collective, the archetypes have no organizing, structuring propensity of their own but appear titanically as compulsion or mass, formless energy. Organization is split off and arranged from above by system and dictatorial edict. The split is between an organizing, forming aspect of the psyche, on one level, and a formless mass energy on another. One can see this split in analysands with Hitler dreams, where a highly structured, dictatorial – perhaps paranoid – ruling principle lays down the law for the rest of the psyche which, as a result, is a formless mass.

The second collective Jung refers to is less dramatic – in fact, the danger of this collectivity is in its comfortable, apparently harmless character. Within these adaptive collective patterns or aspects of oneself and the world, consciousness appears sleepily unaware. One is carried along by habitual social patterns, pre-established structures – those attitudes and values with which the individual psyche has not actually worked or grappled. Thus the psyche moves sheeplike along paths others have formed, the usual, most natural, easiest routes.

Aesthetically, to work in this natural, comfortable mode would be like crafting a painting or poem in the most conventional manner with mediocre, though perhaps acceptable, results. The key to recognizing sheeplike collectivity is uniformity. The forms, styles, techniques are all the same and in tune with the times, the present structure of things, present values. We all live to some extent in this mode, for conformity can free our energy for other things, and besides we need something of this "forgetful attitude" from which to work.

The third manner in which Jung uses the term "the collective" is the most important. This collectivity is the grounding of his thought. At the deepest reaches of the psyche, this collective points to human potentiality; it is the source of creativity, universal values, and archetypal possibilities. Unlike the first collective, which appears *en masse*, or the second, which is merely going along, this third sense of the collective displays inherent formal properties. In an individuation process, the psyche comes to terms and works with these collective forms and contents, so that in the (ideal) end, one is not only unique but also most connected with collective – by which Jung here means commonly shared, universal, archetypal – qualities; one is in touch with the deepest levels of others as well as oneself.

When in our training programs we speak of the necessity to maintain a "tension with the collective" – if we are referring to this deepest collective of commonality with others – then by tension we mean the deepest tension of the individuation process, which requires the sacrifice of ego narrowness, self-interest, and pettiness to larger, broader values and concerns. Collectivity in this third sense is very much connected with Jung's notion of the self. In fact, if "the self" be an isolated figure in a tower, it is not a self at all (but, rather, an inflated ego).

The collective as humanity and its shared values has nothing to do with standardization, networks of rules, or with any fixed notion of society. As an ingredient in the individuation process, this collectivity is an achievement by way of the unique: it begins with the unique tensions of a particular soul. It is a work from within an individual psyche and the results of the psyche coming to terms with its own necessities. This collectivity is both a natural process (given with the nature of the psyche, the nature of being human) and a great work, an achievement. To relate *commonly* by means of one's *individuality* is thus a goal of the process. But, I repeat, to achieve this collective engagement, it is essential that one *begin with the individual*, with the particular. Then the collective shows immediately, irrepressibly, in whatever one is working with. Every psyche is in a collective setting, but this collective is always particularized – in a room, a family, a city. In other words, the collective manifests itself within a setting of particular significance, a setting that has psychological importance. We recognize the collective not by a general idea, but as it actually impinges. For one individual, the collective may show in his inability to connect with his family; for another, the inability to talk with the gas station attendant or to use public toilets. If we look for the collective in what we *expect* as collective, we may miss where the collective is actually, most importantly present.

So although everything exists within a collective, it is best not to define from the outside or in general what that collectivity necessarily is. Whenever we say that the collective must necessarily be some set of rules or standardized structures, then we are no longer working from the individual psyche and its processes. We are no longer beginning with the work and how it frames itself. Further, by standardizing our notion of the collective, we have shifted from Jung's deepest sense of commonality to the more superficial notions with which individuation feels itself in conflict.

I believe this conflict was going on in Jung. When he made his vehement attacks against collective standardization, perhaps it was not only Nazi Germany he was reacting against, but also psychologically he was fighting for the right of his originality, which led to the founding of a psychology based on the individual in his or her psychological reality. That which Freud called the reality principle for Jung – as I read him – began with and proceeded out of *psychic* reality.

This tension between external, collective adaptation (the systematized and "most natural" route) and the discovery of one's unique mode of commonality is a dynamic of the Shadow – or rather, of two Shadows, as though conflict within the Shadow itself were necessary to generate psychic tension. One Shadow, unconsciously adaptive and conforming, follows the most natural route to avoid consciousness or trouble. The second Shadow is a miscreant that disturbs, irritates, does not fit in, is not satisfied with the status quo. This Shadow embraces the unique for the sake of the unique and, through symptoms, oddities, and unconscious slips, goads the psyche into continuous movement.

To connect these Shadow dynamics with practical matters of training – one of the issues now agitating some Jungian groups is whether to require that trainees be licensed. Licensing is an eminently practical, reasonable, sensibly adaptive move. The conformist Shadow has no difficulty understanding the advantages: one can receive referrals; one is respectable and so can be employed by agencies and institutions; analysands can pay with insurance money. One can build a large practice. The advantages are so great that even the miscreant Shadow would enjoy the shelter it offers (the better to work his mischief). Licensing for him, too, is preferable but only insofar as the paths leading to licensing do not compromise his egregious sense of the odd, unusual, and individual. For that reason he may have trouble with academic psychology, a field based on scientific thinking, the principle of parsimony, generalities, and statistical averages. Within this way of thinking, the miscreant Shadow loses his purposeful function within the psyche and becomes merely a variation of the statistical norm.

But here I, too, may be guilty of generalizing. In truth there are individuals for whom this kind of scientific training is in keeping with their Shadow dynamics, their inner processes. The real problem, I suppose, comes only when this adaptive Shadow turns solar, moves into power, and forgets then its nature as Shadow, i.e., as dark, distinct, multiple, and particular. When the Shadow claims itself as sun principle, claims its unique processes as general rule, then we get dicta and their systems and networks of unbendable rules. Then the self-organizing power of the psychological is lost, and we are no longer working aesthetically from deeper levels of collective potentiality.

One of the characteristics of the Shadow turned solar is that it sees reality in the harshest glare of sunlight. Requirements, rules, and accepted patterns must be followed directly and literally, whereas from a darker, more shadowy point of view, the world itself is in the shadows. Reality is not just one hard-edged thing, but multiple things in softer hues. And there are indirect, sensitive, moonlit ways of moving through and with a gentler, more imaginative world. One need not project all one's tensions with the collective onto the literal world of the fathers above. Psychologically there may be many more fertile realms of tension.

One of these realms, ironically, may be the tensions that exist among us as Jungians. It seems to me that Jung's psychology is broad, complex, and rich enough to hold many differences. These differences and differentiations, regionally and individually, are our fertility. Thank heavens, Jung never laid out a clear, noncontradictory system. Because his psychology is based on the individuation process, diversity is crucial. The greater danger for our discipline is not where we disagree, but where we agree; for where we agree, we have no chance to recognize Shadow. Where we agree we become organized, systematized – the collective entity against which Jung always warned.

By way of summary let me list some implications for training:

(1) The more we acquire dogmatic rules and elaborate systems for our training programs, the more we move toward international standardization, an external unity in which we all would have the same training requirements – the more we lose our particular value and uniqueness, regionally and individually.

(2) In order to improve quality in training, we might best cultivate a sharper, more differentiated perception of the individual. Our present emphasis upon quantity in training (requiring increasingly greater numbers of hours) does not necessarily meet this need. In fact, quantitative thinking may be obscuring the real need.

(3) As our numbers grow, the need to protect ourselves against charlatanism increases. But, as Adolf Guggenbühl has pointed out, the charlatan is within us all.[119] Thus, the best safeguard against charlatanism is a training that makes essential a detailed, differentiated Shadow awareness. Early on I called this an aesthetic training and said I did not mean necessarily a literal training in the arts. True, an exact

119 See A. Guggenbühl-Craig, *Power in the Helping Professions* (Putnam, Conn.: Spring Publications, 2008).

eye and ear for individuality and differences can be developed in clinical work as well as through a training in the liberal arts or humanities. Indeed, this perception could be developed in any number of different educational disciplines or apart from them all. What one has studied would seem less important than the eye one has developed. Further, since Shadow arises with each stance or position, it is crucial for us to disagree and to diversify.

(4) If we keep individual differences ever before us, in our training and among ourselves, those differences will not be forced to conglobulate and split off. What is actually happening when there is emphasis on unification and standardization is that a countermovement is being constellated. Talk of uniformity is destroying our unity. For the Jungian mind, uniformity and unity do not mix easily.

Were we to agree to differ, that is, to agree upon individuality, we would effect a much stronger binding among us – a binding based not so much upon one kind of Shadow raised to solar consciousness, with its resulting programs and procedures. By agreeing to differ, we would more likely keep our unity, since our true Jungian commonality is rooted in each of us as individuals.

Rules of Thumb Toward an Archetypal Psychology Practice

The other day I was asked if I still considered myself an archetypal psychologist. The question astonished me. How could I not? I was in at the base level before archetypal psychology was named "archetypal psychology" – first as student *adept*, later as *soror mystica*, leaning over the edge with those stirring this heady brew. Newts, lizards, our innards were all in the pot. Not only did I feel archetypal psychology was me, I was part it – in it for a toe or two, my whole head and lots of spit.

Yet it is true, in the last several years I have not hung out much with the folks talking archetypal psychology. One of the reasons for my absence is that as archetypal discussion has become focused increasingly on ideas, I have become increasingly less so. I certainly honor ideation; theory is important. No school of anything would exist without it. But it is not for all of us – all the time. As I age, I become more often "hands on" about most things. This does not mean I don't think – only that when I do, the thoughts tend to appear clothed as psychological dynamics, mechanisms, appearing in individuals, relationships, groups, or even situations. This practice of seeing ideas as they function is fun stuff for me, and that's where I have spent my time. Is that still archetypal psychology? Well, you tell me. Perhaps it is just my archetypal psychology, one of the many archetypal psychologies. Whatever the case, in the following pages I will lay out something of how I have come to think. These are my rules of thumb for practice, as well as I can describe them just now.

Rule of Thumb #1: *Any Idea Can Be Used Defensively*

Here by "rule of thumb" I mean: approximately, or more or less. Seems to me there are no "right" ideas, more or less. The "less" part is that some ideas truly *are* more useful, rich, fruitful, interesting, promising. Ah, but that doesn't mean they are right – or wrong either, for that matter.

As a depth psychologist, my focus is on how the psyche works. One of the ways the psyche works, according to depth psychology, is by way of a fragile ego fending off what it perceives to be threats from within or without. To protect itself against these threats, the ego hauls from its arsenal all sorts of defensive weaponry.

Ideas are like the ramparts surrounding the castle. They are designed to keep other ideas from intruding. In times of peace they may give lovers a safe place to meet, wise men a space to converse above the treetops without interruption, a place for women to spin in the fresh air, and wizards to conjure under the stars. But in times of war, ramparts are used to hide behind while arrows fly and boulders are catapulted. So, too, with ideas. Ideas can nurture life, or they can serve as defensive structures.

Rule of Thumb # 2: *If a Sacred Cow Is Blocking the Path, Shoo It Off*

Depth psychology assumes a reality called the unconscious. The "un" part of the unconscious refers to that which is not, not conscious, unknown. Making the unconscious conscious, in the Freudian sense, or (in more modern Jungian terms) integrating unconscious contents and dynamics into more workable positions, adding resources, complexity, and richness to the personality – that is certainly a goal of depth psychological work. The means for accomplishing this work requires continual seeing through.

The method of depth psychology is something of a *via negativa*. By that I mean we more often shoo away what is blocking the path than claim to know what the path ought actually be. Nonetheless there are some general values assumed, although they may vary in emphasis depending upon the context and from practitioner to practitioner. Some of these values are: the unknown, depth, resonance, complexity, interconnection, integration, richness, mastery. I'm sure you can add others.

Values or value-laden concepts can provide orientation, but one must sense and consciously choose when one or another set of values is to be applied. When values are clung to, one tends to get lost in their glow such that one can no longer discern the more subtle, new, challenging, or, I would even say, real psychic events. When one or another value-laden feeling is embraced such that the ego hides behind it, then we may need to put aside the value itself, shoo it off the path, even if that value reeks of Truth and Motherhood – or Soul, Psyche, and World. Whatever the sacred terms, the secret handclasps, such values can and will be used to occlude more more interesting, challenging or fecund developments in psychological life.

Rule of Thumb #3: *Ideas Ought Not Be Applied*

The problem with the notion of praxis is that we tend to think of it as an application of theory. When we apply ideas to practical situations, I find it usually results in misapplication of one sort or another. In fact, the first few times around, misuse is almost a given. A new idea is like a new tool or toy one might try out in many places – most of which are not appropriate. In my experience, few life situations are such that a single idea does them justice.

My view is that it is best to work from the event to the idea not the other way round. (1) Begin with the living event, that is, the image; (2) focus on the image/event, sensing into it; and (3) track bits of resonance that begin to form out of the event. Whether these resonances are immediately like known ideas or mere fragments does not matter. Eventually ideas will spring up like weeds around and through them.

Ideas are organic. They live in things, sort of like William Carlos Williams's "red wheel barrel glazed with rain." [120] Maybe here the rain is the fragments, the glimmers of shimmering ideas.

---

120 See above, 101 n 63.

Rule of Thumb #4: *When Possible, Think Poetically*

For Aristotle, practicality, or *praxis*, leads to action, whereas making, or *poeisis*, leads to production. Aside from *praxis* as in a spiritual practice, which, to my mind, is right on the money, *praxis* tends to lend itself more to political thinking. Marx regarded his dialectical materialism as *praxis*. Sometimes, however, one is more about making – simply making – than about politics. When that is the case, as it frequently is for me, the fantasy of making, creating – just the activity for the sake of itself – is quite appealing. For me, "making" psychological moves, interpretations, interventions, reflections, and moments seems more fitting than any other conceptualization for what I am about.

Rule of Thumb #5: *Go Connatural*

Connaturality is a term coined by the Catholic theologian Jacques Maritain. Maritain was interested in the interrelation between artistic processes and the processes of nature. In his view, the task of the artist or craftsman is to align mimetically with "nature's secret workings and inner ways."[121] He saw artistic activity, when working properly, as attempting to parallel nature's processes. Human creativity is like nature's creativity. The task is to work connaturally with nature on a very conscious level – to sense nature's operations, to feel them, see them, hear them. The attempt to look deeply into natural psychological processes, attuning with what is perceived, is what depth psychology is all about.

Rule of Thumb #6: *Symbols Are Not Symbols Of Anything But Symbolic With Many Things*

The Islamic scholar Henry Corbin characterized symbols as "symbolizing with" rather than "symbolic to" their referents.[122] The distinction

---

121 J. Maritain, *Creative Intuition in Art and Poetry* (Princeton Univ. Press, 1953), 127.

122 H. Corbin, *Avicenna and the Visionary Recital*, trans. W. R. Trask (New York: Pantheon, 1960), 261. See also "*Mundus Imaginalis*, of the Imaginary and the Imaginal," trans. R. Horine, *Spring 1972: An Annual of Archetypal Psychology and Jungian Thought*, 9.

is important in that no one symbol is regarded as necessarily prior to or more important than another. The kind of making implied here would develop by way of similarities, reverberations, and improvisations mimetic with, or paralleling natural movements and processes. In that same spirit, rather like the spirit of Maritain's connaturality, our depth psychological work proceeds with an ear to the ground of nature's reverberations, both natural and symbolic.

Rule of Thumb # 7: *Stick to the Image*

Ok, so this is an old rule. We all know it. I have always attributed it to Rafael López-Pedraza, since he was the guy I heard it from repeatedly. At this point in my life, however, my sense may have wandered a bit from Rafael's. Today I regard image as a more flexible notion than I once did. One way to understand its adaptability is to talk about framing.

Rule of Thumb # 8: *To Know It Is to Frame It*

Please, let me be clear. I am not saying things exist *only* because of their framing. I *am* saying that frames organize what we see. Organized well, what we see can become fresh, even breathtaking. The way in which a picture is framed becomes part of its effect and meaning. The frame of the window over my desk gives a particular view of the woods outside. When I frame a picture in my camera viewfinder, I am positioning the view in such a way as to enable something revelatory to come forth. In a moving image, many frames rushing one after another become the film that an editor then cuts and shapes – that is, frames – into the final film. The purpose of framing is to put limits on the view so that what is within those limits can be focused on with greater clarity and freshness.

How we frame a story we tell to a friend or a case presentation to colleagues has to do with what we want to show (and perhaps how we want it and ourselves to be seen). How we frame something also conditions how others approach it, what they get from it, and what activities generate around it. This is not as obvious as it may seem. In a case colloquium, for example, someone presents a situation with a client with whom they are having difficulty. Generally speaking, what the participants in the group will see, being astute psychological participants, is not what the presenter "meant" for them to see but what the presenter has not presented and perhaps not known.

I consider the image here to be both what the presenter presented and what others saw, the unconscious workings behind the presentation and evoked by it. The conscious framing was the framing of the presentation, but that framing also brought other levels, other insights, and other points of view into the discussion.

If the practitioner had presented the story differently, what the participants perceived would have also been somewhat different. Let's say the practitioner had framed the story, beginning and end, with a statement about how annoyed he gets with this particular patient. The group would then tend to work on the case with this countertransference emotion in mind. My point is that situations framed differently are different, and the comments as well as the dynamics of the group will change accordingly – because the image is different.

Sometimes images are framed too small. When too little context is given a situation, working with it tends to get loose, projective, less fitting, and less meaningful in terms of the actual situation. On the other hand, sometimes psychological events get framed so large that it is difficult to work on them in depth or with anything but broad, sweeping strokes. On occasion these large strokes are just what you want, as, for example, when taking on issues at a cultural or political level. At this level, particular and precise image work is not helpful or appropriate.

Rule of Thumb #9: *The Observer and Observed May or May Not Be the Same*

Our perceptual convention is to experience ourselves when we observe – for example, the participants observing the case presentation (as we discussed above – as separate from what we are observing. We know from modern physics, phenomenology, and other disciplines, that we are, in one way or another, implicated in what we observe. But on a practical level, the positions we assume vis-à-vis "other" – whatever "other" is (dream, client, colleagues, the world of psychology) varies considerably.

Sometimes it is important to be close to the "other," so close as nearly to merge. With a client's dream, say, some therapists might want to be so close that they feel the dream's energies through their own muscles and organs. They might then speak to the dream via their own imaginations. Their imaginings (or amplifications or associations, for that matter) may be as important to the process as the patient's imaginings.

Or one may assume a position at some distance from the patient and the material. It is not that one or another stance is correct; each has advantages and can be more or less fitting depending on the circumstances. Sometimes it is useful to get as close as you can to the experience. At other times, it is crucial to put yourself out of the picture so you can see it more clearly. What's important here is to know that you are assuming positions, and to attempt to develop as large a repertoire as possible. In any situation, you can then consciously choose your stance, which includes of course knowing the effects of that position, its strengths, its limitations and its dangers.

Sometimes one wishes to frame what is going on in, let's say, a therapeutic situation, in terms of "transference/countertransference dynamics." When one frames the situation within this conceptual fantasy, one can see everything as occurring within and because of those relations. To pass exams in many Jungian training institutes nowadays, one must be adept at this mode of framing and at use of the language that goes with it. As with any other frame, this transference enclosure both limits and reveals. To my mind, the danger of this model is that it is the currently accepted one, and so is usually assumed to be "true" and taken literally.

Rule of Thumb # 10: *Contrast: It's a Set Up*

I find James Hillman's notion of multiplicity to be not only a larger, more generous umbrella, but also a more interesting attitude than, for example, dualism. Yet, at times, one wants to point up strong contrasts. On such occasions one might sound "either/or" dualistic. Contrasts are ways of making points stand out clearly. Imagine a painting with a dark background and white figures in the foreground. The white figures stand out because of the contrasting background. When archetypal psychology sets up oppositions, it is important to remember that these oppositions are about contrast rather than literal exclusion. Think of some of archetypal psychology's oppositions: underworld versus the day world, imaginal versus heroic ego, world versus consulting room, and (my favorite) psychological versus literal. The good guys are set up at one end of the opposition and the bad guys at the other, good guys foreground, bad guys background.

Aesthetically speaking, these "either/or" exclusions create contrasts to make a point. But, let's not forget, these bad guys are merely straw men hauled in to be railed against. In drama, straw men caricatures act as foils for the more complex principle characters. Some dramatists I know maintain that collective taste requires these figures. Maybe so, but as psychologists we need to remember that it is a set-up.

Rule of Thumb #11: *Steal Tools When Necessary*

Hillman characterized his psychological method as like that of a *brico-leur* (an inventive do-it-yourselfer); I'd say mine is like a thief, though a good thief and for good reasons, I hope. Although archetypal psychology distinguishes itself philosophically from widespread collective psychologies such as behaviorism or cognitive psychology, nonetheless as a practitioner one might on occasion lift a tool or two from their bright boxes. On occasion, those toolboxes may contain something useful. The tool may be one that allows us to focus on behavior as such, or to advocate change in behavior before understanding what the behavior is about. This may sound quite unlike depth psychology, but it is sometimes necessary – as in situations of abuse or addiction. Since there are as many explanations of events as there are psychological perspectives for viewing them, sometimes a simple negative reinforcement (such as terminating the therapy) is the way to go.

If we take seriously the Maritain/Corbin image of parallel processes, then perhaps imaginal change can begin with behavioral change as well as the other way around. Sometimes grabbing the stick by the other end is easier. It seems to me, it is not other psychologies that are reductive, material, and literal – *it is we who are, whenever we view them without a psychological eye.*

If we stand on psychic ground, *in media res*, maintaining our awareness from that position, what we do will be psychologically based. It is a matter of awareness. When we are psychologically aware, our means will be metaphorical, and our tools reflective.

Rule of Thumb # 12: *Don't Take the Literal Literally*

Earlier I said that the literal versus the psychological was my favorite opposition. But, you know, one ought not take even the literal so literally. To do so is to become way too literal. That literal voice, insisting on "nothing but," is just one of many voices in the chorus. Sometimes it is useful for belting out strong, sure tones, but the point is to hear it as one voice – rather than the whole-truth, nothing-but-the-truth it pretends to be.

Rule of Thumb #13: *Truth or* Daimon

Sometimes I think of truth imagistically, as in the "true line" a carpenter might determine, a navigator reckon, or a Zen master draw in the sand. True is for me of highest value, but I do not capitalize the word. In terms of an individual psyche, I think of truth as the path of individuation. This old-fashioned Jungian term is sufficiently vague, subjective, and interior to work for me. Some might speak of following one's *daimon* rather than Jung's notion of *individuation* as a guide, but *daimons* are flashy. Besides *daimons* are also demons, and so easy to identify with! So, too, notions like "psyche" and soul don't work for me as they once did. In the beginning of archetypal psychology these words were truly alive, earth-shaking, electrifying, daring as heck. Now they are clichés in the titles of half the books on the self-help shelves. Is the notion (psyche, soul) true? Sure. But it is hard nowadays to inspire in someone like me much feeling of a true line from those words.

I tend to orient myself with more practical aesthetic notions like "what works." What "works" as a novel, film, painting, or piece of music is determined by the piece itself. Each piece sets up its own criteria. In this way the work is measured against itself– sort of like what individuation implies in personal psychology, where the unique nature of the person is the goal.

Rule of Thumb # 14: *Layard's Rule*

I tend to view dreams through Layard's rule.[123] I may not always share
this vision with my client. But I often do, because it is in fact how I see
things. John Layard was an anthropologist and a first generation Jungian
analyst who resided in England. James Hillman passed along the maxim
to me almost forty years ago, crediting it to Layard, and so I do also. This
rule of thumb has since served me and several generations of students
well. It is my favorite tool.

The rule goes like this: "Everything in the dream is right except perhaps the dream ego." The purpose of this rule of thumb is to turn awareness toward a realm beyond the ego. Its use deliteralizes the usual, ego
point of view, enabling a change in perspective.

As with any other rule of thumb, this one applies only loosely and
sometimes not at all. Always it is, I think, a helpful perspective for prac-
titioners in deepening their own awareness. It is not always the right tool
for the therapy. In some cases – for example, when support or stabiliza-
tion is a priority – moving against the ego perspective is not smart therapeutically. In such instances, Layard's rule is not the right tool. Pick up
another. As with any other rule, this one is simply more or less useful
and appropriate – one of many in the tool box.

As an example, let's look at the following dream:

> I go into my bathroom. My dog, Max, is in the bathtub, under water.
> He is just lying there like he usually lies. I am horrified, knowing he is
> going to drown. He just looks up at me as if nothing is wrong.

I know nothing about the woman who dreamt this dream – her situation in life, her complexes, where she is in her analytic process – nothing. But that does not mean I cannot get something from the dream.

From a naturalistic perspective (the ego perspective here), the dog
seems as though he is going to drown, and that feels terrible to the
dreamer. To apply the Layard rule, however (here, an underwater as
well as "underworld" perspective), we bracket out the ego's feeling and

---

123 See also above, 80.

look to the dog. Max acts as though nothing is wrong. Perhaps this is an underwater dog, able to survive under water. Or perhaps he is going to drown, to dissolve into the alchemical *solutio*, and that is part of the process. Whatever the case, we know clearly from the dog's point of view, according to Layard, that indeed "nothing is wrong." Everything is as it should be.

This point of view would seem horrific to an ego- or humanistically-oriented psychologist on several counts. For one thing, the situation is not natural. Dogs are not naturally content underwater. Thus there is something wrong with this woman's "dog." Her dog instinct is un-aware, self-destructive. Another reason the dream would not sit well is that in humanistic psychology it is the human that is most highly valued. Human perspectives and values are identified with and taken literally.

To flip things such that we are looking from the dog's perspective, trusting the animal over the human viewpoint, can lead us into aware-nesses that other, more usual perspectives do not allow. The Layard perspective deepens and enriches our understanding. If everything is right except the dream ego, it is "right" that the dog dies. Perhaps the dog is like an old instinct, effective for many years in sniffing out what was what, but no longer needed. Perhaps a new dog with new senses is in order.

Rule of Thumb # 15: *Listen to Your Friends, Love Your Teacher*

I regularly lead seminars for students in the final stages of depth psycho-logical study. The drill is that each student takes several hours during the weekend to talk about their work with a client.

As the participants interact around the images and processes that arise, I am astonished at how well they have come to understand one another. Of course, each arrives at the weekend with particular perspec-tives and favorite theories. They may not always agree, but eventually they all come to appreciate one another, to understand what is being said and it is coming from. They listen to one another – and to me.

Do they know I am an archetypal psychologist? Do they know my background? I don't know. If they do know, certainly not in any detail.

Yet they are doing what I consider to be archetypal psychology. They are focusing carefully on what appears as image, aware of their framing, the lenses they use. They bracket causal explanations and appreciate mimetic resonances. They have learned to steal. They make inventive use of available resources (the *bricoleur*!). To one degree or another each has an eye for some "true" line. They recite Layard's Rule like a mantra. Is this archetypal psychology? Well, it is certainly one form of it.

Thank you, James Hillman. Those years in the mix with you were fundamental to my learning, glorious in reach and spread and lift, beyond inspirational. It was an extraordinary ride. I remain deeply and forever grateful to you, my teacher.